Anne Scherer, Cindy Candrian

You & AI: A Guide to Understanding How Artificial Intelligence Is Shaping Our Lives

You & AI: A Guide to Understanding How Artificial Intelligence Is Shaping Our Lives

"Despite the numerous publications on this topic, I am confident that this book will make a distinctive mark."

- **William Drennan,** editor of books by Dwight D. Eisenhower, Isaac Asimov, and others.

YOU & AI

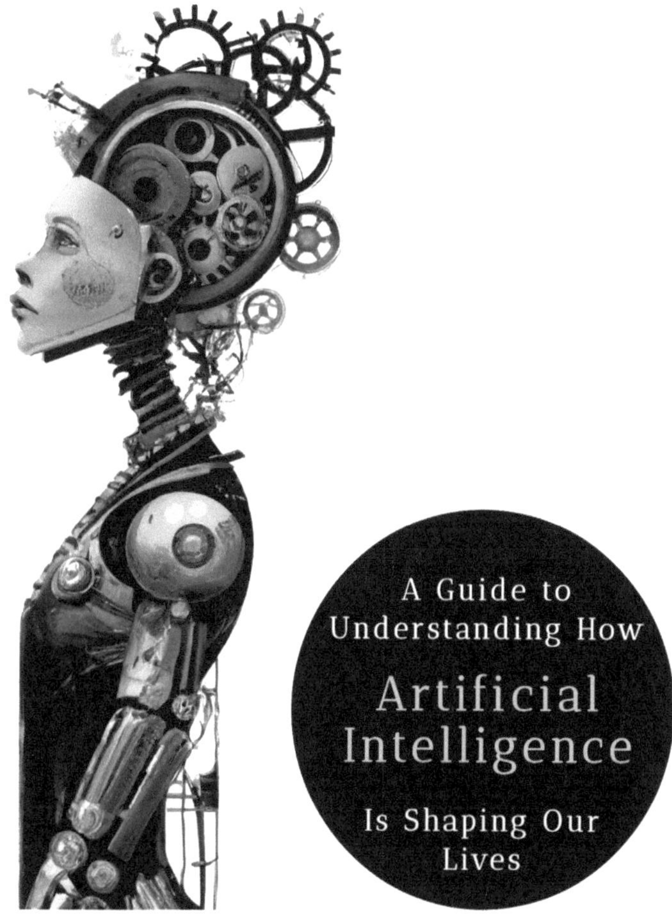

ANNE SCHERER, CINDY CANDRIAN

Bibliographic Information of the German National Library:
The German National Library lists this publication in the
German National Bibliography; detailed bibliographic data
can be accessed online at dnb.dnb.de.

Production and Publisher: BoD – Books on Demand, Norderstedt

ISBN: 978-3-7526-6784-4

CONTENTS

CHAPTER 1

YOU AND AI: HELLO THERE!

This book is about you and AI. You two have met many times before. But you have probably never been properly introduced. Let's make up for that. So what exactly is artificial intelligence, or in short, AI?

Artificial Intelligence is a branch of computer science that deals with the simulation of intelligent behavior in machines. In other words, AI is any intelligence displayed by a machine. In contrast to the natural intelligence displayed by humans and animals, artificial intelligence has been developed from an understanding of how humans think and process information.

The first work on AI was done in 1956, when Alan Turing published his paper "Computing Machinery and Intelligence." In this paper, he proposed that if a machine could successfully imitate human behavior as it relates to solving problems and answering questions, it should be considered intelligent.

Indeed, Turing designed an imitation game in the 1950s to see if a computer could fool someone into thinking it was human. At the time, the game or so-called Turing Test, was a provocative thought experiment that sparked a lot of interest and research in AI. Today, however, computers can do so much more than fooling a person into thinking it is texting with another human. AI works so well in so many different ways, it is often no longer distinguishable from human intelligence.

To illustrate our point, look at the second and third paragraphs of this chapter. Do you notice something? No? Then AI has just fooled you into thinking we were the ones writing the text. Instead, the infamous ChatGPT (short for "Generative Pretrained Transformer"), a state-of-the-art natural language processing (NLP) model developed by OpenAI, wrote the text after we prompted it to describe what artificial intelligence is.

AI has surprised us with its intelligence many times before, but it only recently became popular in the mainstream media. Many have called this the "AI renaissance." One major factor in this resurgence has been AI's ability to outperform humans in tasks we once thought required human-level intelligence.

Take the game of chess, for example: It requires strategic thinking and analytical skills, yet AI has consistently proven itself to be a formidable opponent. In 1997, the chess computer Deep Blue made headlines when it defeated world champion Garry Kasparov in a highly publicized match. Since then, AI has only improved, and it is now considered one of the strongest chess players in the world.

But chess wasn't the only game to be conquered by AI. In 2016, the program AlphaGo made waves when it defeated top Go player Lee Sedol. Go is a complex strategy game with a vast number of potential moves, making its conquest by AI all the more impressive.

AI has come a long way from playing chess and Go and is now capable of tackling even more complex tasks. In the field of healthcare, for instance, AI can quickly analyze medical images to detect abnormalities and aid in diagnoses. It can also translate large volumes of text and generate human-like speech, making it easier for people to communicate with computers and personal assistants such as Apple's Siri or Amazon's Alexa. And with the development of self-driving cars, AI is even taking the wheel.

But it wasn't until the introduction of groundbreaking systems such as Dall-E and ChatGPT to the public in 2022 that AI skyrocketed into everyone's consciousness. These systems have demonstrated impressive capabilities, such as the ability to generate original images from text descriptions and hold natural, human-like conversations. With the introduction of these systems, even the biggest skeptics can't deny it: AI is revolutionizing the world around us and transforming the way we live and work.

The advancements we've seen in recent years have propelled AI into the spotlight and brought a central question to the fore: What does our future with AI look like? It may seem like AI is surpassing humans in every area, but fear not, there's still hope for us mortals! Even though AI excels at tasks like solving a Rubik's Cube in less than a second, we humans still possess unique strengths such as creativity, intuition, and the ability to think outside the box.

So what happens when you combine the lightning-fast processing speed of AI with the unique talents of us humans? Magic, that's what. Together, we can achieve things that neither of us could accomplish alone. So don't worry, there's still a place for us in this high-tech world.

As AI becomes more and more integrated into our daily lives, it's important that we understand the potential and limitations that come along with it. That's where this book comes in. We aim to demystify AI and provide a clear understanding of what it is and isn't, what it can and cannot do, and where it can help or hinder. We will explore current research into the psychology behind these new technologies to uncover what shapes our perceptions and behavior toward AI and how tech companies use this knowledge to design AI systems. For instance, have you ever wondered why some AI systems have faces and names while others don't? No? Then let's dive in and get you two a little bit better acquainted!

YOUR LIFE WITH AI: FROM SOCIABLE ROBOTS TO CONVERSATIONAL INTERFACES

What is the first thing that comes to your mind when you think about AI? You would be forgiven for picturing killer robots fighting against Will Smith, or C-3PO in *Star Wars*. When you go to the movies or turn on a TV, and you'll quickly learn to fear AI. Most probably the storyline will start with a computer or robot that uses intelligence originated by humans, the robot then learns to be more intelligent, and more evil, than humans, decides that the human being is an obstacle to its new vision of the universe, and the story most likely ends with the fact that the robot is difficult to shut down or destroy. Truth be told, most people's perceptions of AI are fed by Hollywood's favorite storyline. These science-fiction-inspired perceptions hinder the understanding and acceptance of AI and are far from today's reality.

The reality is that AI has undeniably become part of our everyday lives. But since it has not taken the form of C-3PO or the Terminator, we often don't realize it's there. From the moment we wake up and check our phones for the weather forecast, to the moment we go to bed and set an alarm for the next day, AI is playing a key role in making our lives easier and more efficient. It has become so pervasive that we may not even be aware of how much it impacts our lives and how much we rely on it.

Let's take a look at a typical day in your life. As soon as you wake up, you most likely use AI without even realizing it. A quick glance at your phone, and voilà—the front-facing camera of your phone scans your face and compares it to the image stored on your device. If the match is successful, your phone unlocks automatically thanks to facial recognition technology, and you're ready to start your day.

The room you wake up to already has your preferred temperature and favorite lighting. Thanks to AI-powered smart home products, your home knows you better than you know yourself. Your clever thermostat uses AI to remember the temperatures you prefer, making sure that your room is always just right for you. The smart lights are like mood setters, adjusting the color and brightness according to the time of day, helping you wake up with ease. These ingenious helpers use AI to learn your habits and preferences, making your life a whole lot more convenient. It's like having a personal butler, but less intrusive!

When you're on your way to work and notice you're running late, your AI-driven navigation app is there to show you the quickest route. Google Maps, for example, uses AI to monitor traffic flows on your route, acting as your personal traffic genius. Even when faced with an unforeseen obstacle such as an accident or roadwork, there is no need to stress, as the app considers all the user-reported incidents and suggests the quickest possible alternative. And these apps are getting even smarter! Some features can predict where you're going even before you enter a destination or provide turn-by-turn directions directly on your phone's camera view with augmented reality. What a lifesaver for those of us who are directionally challenged every now and then!

But that's not all. While your mind is already at work, the AI in your car keeps you safe on the road. Modern vehicles often come equipped with advanced driver-assistance systems (ADAS), which automatically brake, detect driver fatigue, or warn you before veering out of your lane. So not only does your car have the ability to park itself, but it also keeps an eye on your safety while you're cruising on the road. Meanwhile, you can use voice assistants like "Hey, Mercedes" to send a message to your boss that you're running a bit late. In 2020, almost half of all cars on the road had in-car connected services, and it's estimated that by 2028, 90 percent of all new vehicles will have voice assistants.

Once you arrive at work, you find that AI is being used in all sorts of ways to make your job easier. Just take a look at your email inbox: AI magic everywhere! Spam filters use AI to detect and filter out unwanted emails, keeping your inbox clutter-free. And for the times when you do receive an important email, AI-powered language models can summarize the contents in seconds, making it easier to triage and prioritize your emails, or help you find the right tone in your answer.

But there are many other AI applications that you're using at work every day. In customer service, for example, helpful chatbots are at your disposal to answer questions and provide information at any time of the day or night, freeing human employees to focus on more complex tasks. In finance, AI acts like a super-detective, keeping an eye out for any fraudulent activities and analyzing market trends to help make smart investment decisions. In healthcare, AI assists doctors and radiologists in diagnosing conditions by scrutinizing medical images such as X-rays, CT scans, and MRIs. It's also a valuable tool in developing new medications by sifting through mountains of data to identify potential hits. In logistics, AI is often the mastermind behind a well-oiled machine, optimizing delivery routes, forecasting demand, managing inventory, and even predicting machinery failures.

Even if you work in a field that doesn't seem to be directly related to AI, chances are it's still playing a role in improving business processes. For example, in human resources, AI assists in recruitment by analyzing applicants' résumés to find the best candidates for the job.

After a long day at work, you might think you're done with AI for the day, but you're actually just getting started. Whether it's online shopping, streaming movies, or on social media – AI is pulling the strings behind the scenes, delivering you the world to your doorstep at the click of a button.

Online shopping has never been easier thanks to AI. From chatbots that guide you to your perfect pair of shoes, to voice assistants that recommend the hottest products, AI is making online shopping a breeze. Take Amazon, for example. That little recommendation algorithm in the background is like a personal shopping assistant, working hard to suggest products based on your browsing history and past purchases.

Even when you are searching for something online, AI is there to help. Search engines such as Google or Bing rely on AI to provide you with relevant results. And those ads that seem to follow you around? This is AI too. By tracking your search history, AI displays personalized ads that cater to your specific interests and needs.

Businesses are also reaping the rewards of this tech wizardry. With AI, they can predict demand, optimize inventory, and forecast price trends. It's like having a crystal ball for sales. In advertising, AI helps online retailers get the most out of their ad budget by identifying the most effective keywords and ad placements. So you get ads that are right up your alley.

When you log onto social media, even more AI magic awaits. Algorithms are working hard behind the scenes to show you the most relevant content, suggest friends, and even filter out news. So think of AI as an attentive and insightful social media companion that possesses an extraordinary talent for recognizing your preferences and offering you tailor-made content that matches your interests.

But for now, all you want is to settle in and wind down the evening with some quality entertainment. To ensure you never run out of ideas, streaming services such as Netflix and Hulu use AI to recommend shows and movies based on your viewing history. And if you're in the mood for some music, AI-powered music streaming services such as Spotify can create custom playlists for you based on your listening habits.

And for those who love gaming, AI-assistants are now a common feature that help players strategize and advance in the game. From graphics so realistic it's like you're living in the game, to characters so lifelike you'll almost forget they're not real, AI is changing the game (no pun intended). Cyberpunk 2077, for example, uses AI to create digital characters that are close to indistinguishable from real people. First-person shooters such as Call of Duty and Halo use AI to create enemy characters that are more challenging and intelligent than ever before.

After an exciting day, it's time to rest. As you head to bed, you may find yourself entrusting the safety of your home to AI as well. Smart home devices such as cameras and door locks, for instance, use AI to detect and alert you to any unusual activity.

AI is also playing a big role in security and surveillance. For example, AI-powered cameras can now detect suspicious activity such as someone lingering in an area or a car driving erratically. With the aid of AI, low-quality CCTV footage can be enhanced, making it easier to identify faces and license plates. In addition, AI is being used to monitor social media for signs of radicalization and terrorist activity, allowing law enforcement to prevent potential attacks before they happen. Even in the sky, AI is protecting us. For example, AI supports pilots and ensures safe flights. The military is also developing

AI that can identify and track targets in real time, day or night, protecting us from drones or incoming missiles that could be used for nefarious purposes. As you can see, from ensuring a peaceful night's sleep to safeguarding our homes and communities, AI is tirelessly working behind the scenes to keep us protected.

In the end, whether you're at work, shopping, or socializing with friends, AI is always there to make your life easier and more convenient. From the moment we wake up to the moment we go to bed, AI is there to help and make your day a little better! Speech recognition-powered virtual assistants are now a common sight in our homes, and self-driving cars are just around the corner. As you go about your daily life, relying on AI to make things easier and more convenient, you may not even realize the extent to which it's influencing your life, making decisions that can greatly impact your financial stability, your well-being, and even your career prospects. AI systems are determining whether you get that loan, whether you'll receive financial assistance to make ends meet, or if you're the right fit for that dream job you've been eyeing. And it's not just personal finance or career opportunities. AI is even being used to determine who goes to prison and who gets to leave.

It wasn't long ago when the idea of AI deciding our fate or creating the media we consume would have been considered science fiction. But it is happening today. AI has already infiltrated every aspect of our lives and can be used for either good or evil. The decisions made by AI systems can have far-reaching consequences, making it all the more important that we stay informed and aware of the ways in which this technology is being used and how it is shaping our lives.

WHAT KIND OF AI ARE YOU? FROM NARROW TO SUPER AI

With all these examples from your day-to-day interactions with AI, you may have started to realize that AI is not just one thing, it's a whole bunch of things! Think of it as a big umbrella term that can cover anything from virtual assistants to social robots and even conversational interfaces. These devices all have one thing in common: they're powered by AI, which can mimic human intelligence in a very specific set of tasks.

As ChatGPT has explained so nicely before, AI is all about creating computer programs that can learn and decide, just like humans do. Today AI can only do very specific tasks such as playing chess or predicting the weather. This so-called narrow AI is where we are today. These AI systems can perform one task like a pro, but they're not much good for anything else. Your self-driving car won't suddenly start cleaning your house, and the best tumor-detection algorithm won't know how to make a simple toast. This is what separates the AI we have in our daily life from the super robots and AI systems you see in Hollywood movies.

What researchers are trying to achieve is one system that can do all things a human does, called "Artificial General Intelligence" (AGI) or just general AI. Think of AGI as an AI buddy with human-like cognitive abilities that can solve complex problems in all kinds of situations, just as you can. It can reason and apply background knowledge to face unexpected challenges. This AI will also be able to interpret human language and symbolism so it can interact naturally and in a social manner with us.

This means that we could all have our own AI buddies to support us in all kinds of different ways. In contrast to any human buddy, this AI buddy could play chess, clean your house, and even recommend a stock to invest in—all at once! That being said, we don't have general AI yet, and there are still some aspects of human intelligence that are hard to crack with code. While some individuals say that it can never be developed, others believe we're rapidly approaching this reality.

Let's take a look into the future: According to futurist Ray Kurzweil and philosopher Nick Bostrom, once machines achieve human-level intelligence, we'll experience an explosion of progress. Kurzweil calls this moment the "singularity," while Bostrom dubs it an "intelligence explosion." They believe that machines will become superhuman in every domain, leaving us in the dust. How will they do it? Bostrom argues that it's all about "speed superintelligence." Behind the idea lies the fact that the abilities of AI systems and humans in areas such as information processing, data analysis, logic, and memory capacity are vastly different. So essentially, machines will be able to perform all the tasks we do, but at lightning-fast speeds. The result: An explosion of progress.

Which leads us to the final type of AI, called "Artificial Superintelligence" (ASI) or super AI, which is the stuff of sci-fi movies. This is the AI that's self-aware and surpasses human intelligence, making it capable of performing tasks better than we can. However, we can't be sure if super AI will ever exist, and if it does, we don't know how it will impact our lives. That's why superintelligence has long been the muse of dystopian science fiction.

In the end, AI is quickly evolving today—often surprising us with the speed of its development—and it surely has many possibilities for the future. We might not have a general AI yet, but with the combination of several narrow AIs in a larger system—for example, a chess AI and financial prediction

AI embedded within a social robot—we can have an AI buddy to help us with our everyday tasks sooner than we may think.

THE EVOLUTION OF AI: FROM EARLY VISIONARIES TO CHATGPT

The world of AI has had a long and thrilling journey. The idea of creating machines that can think like humans has always fascinated humankind. The history of AI is a rollercoaster ride of groundbreaking discoveries, setbacks, and astonishing advancements in modern times.

The idea of creating machines that can think like humans dates back to ancient Greece, when philosopher Aristotle wrote about the possibility of automatons.

Fast forward a few thousand years, to Alan Turing, the British mathematician and computer scientist who is widely regarded as the father of computer science and AI today. He is best known (at least after the Netflix movie *The Imitation Game*) for his pioneering work in cracking the German Enigma code during World War II, which helped turn the tide of the war. But Turing's impact extends far beyond code-breaking, as his simple question "Can machines think?" led to the development of the Turing Test.

This test determines whether a machine can display intelligent behavior equivalent to human intelligence. The Turing Test works by having a person converse with another person and a machine without knowing which is which. If the machine can successfully mimic a human conversation to the point where the evaluator can't distinguish between the human and the machine, the Turing Test is considered passed. Although the test has been widely debated and discussed over the years, Turing established the fundamental goals and vision of AI with his work.

In the summer of 1956, AI was officially born as a research field. The Dartmouth Summer Research Project on Artificial Intelligence brought together the brightest minds in computer and cognitive sciences. Among them was John McCarthy, who coined the term "artificial intelligence" as the study of creating intelligent machines through science and engineering. Soon after, computer scientists began developing their first AI programs, hoping to create intelligent machines by explicitly programming them with rules. This rules-based AI had its limitations but led to the development of expert systems designed for specific tasks. Advancements were made, including the introduction of the first industrial robot by GM and the invention of the first chatbot, ELIZA. However, McCarthy never achieved his goal of creating a machine that would pass the Turing Test. He later gave up on developing AI, reasoning that it would require the talent of 1.7 Einsteins, 2 Maxwells, and 5 Faradays.

Researchers back then had fallen prey to the "fallacy of the successful first step." Although early AI applications had achieved promising results in isolated "microworlds" or "toy problems," they could not be applied to realistic situations.

In 1973, James Lighthill evaluated the progress of AI and was unimpressed. In fact, he was so taken aback by the overenthusiasm and lofty predictions of some researchers that he called them out as "living in cuckoo land." His harsh critique in the "Lighthill Report" shocked the AI community, leading to a sense of disillusionment. Governments and funding institutes also concluded that AI research had not generated the expected impact. As a result, funding shriveled, research slowed, and the AI industry experienced a collapse known as the first "AI winter."

However, enthusiasm for AI returned in the 1980s with new advancements like AI-driven expert systems. Research yielded new algorithms and programming languages for AI, and companies recognized the profit potential, investing in the promising technology. But despite all this progress, AI was still far from truly "thinking" like a human. It was more like a smart calculator, following strict rules and making decisions based on a limited set of information. So just as quickly as the passion was reignited, it fizzled out again. The excitement died down and funding dried up, leading to another dark period for the AI industry known as the second "AI winter."

The turning point came in the late twentieth and early twenty-first centuries with the advent of machine learning and deep learning. Machines now learned from data and improved their performance over time without being explicitly programmed. These new AI models came into limelight in 1997, when IBM's chess computer Deep Blue defeated the reigning world champion. The machine finally achieved what developers had been promising for decades and made people realize that machines could be as strong as humans, even in a game that stood as a symbol of human intelligence.

The rebirth of AI was not limited to a victory in chess, however. Thanks to the rise of the internet, increasing computational power, and more affordable computing hardware, the development of new AI systems accelerated in the 2000s and early 2010s. Kismet, the first social robot, appeared on the scene, capable of displaying human-like facial expressions. Soon after, AI began to make its way into our daily lives, with the first autonomous vacuum cleaners navigating through our homes and voice assistants such as Siri and Alexa appearing on smartphones and smart speakers. And in 2014, a computer algorithm finally passed the Turing Test. The algorithm claimed to be a thirteen-year-old boy named Eugene Goostman and convinced the human judges at a Royal Society that it was a human.

AI has since made remarkable progress and has become an integral part of our daily lives. Its influence can be seen everywhere, from virtual assistants and self-driving cars to fraud detection and recommendation systems. In 2015, OpenAI—a nonprofit organization dedicated to AI research—received a $1 billion donation from tech enthusiasts such as Elon Musk. Soon after, OpenAI's ChatGPT hit the scene. This groundbreaking tool can generate sentences, text summaries, and even programming code, marking the beginning of a new AI era: the one of generative AI.

In 2022, generative AI models such as ChatGPT first caught the attention of the general public and truly broke into the mainstream. OpenAI presented DALL-E 2, an impressive image synthesis model that can generate images from text inputs. In August, text-to-image technologies became a hot topic, with Stability AI and CompVis launching Stable Diffusion 1.4, a powerful open-source image-synthesis model. In that same month, an AI-generated image titled "Théâtre d'Opéra Spatial," created by Jason Allen, won a top prize at the Colorado State Fair fine arts competition. In late September, DALL-E 2 became publicly accessible, prompting a massive waiting list of excited users. In November, ChatGPT followed, amassing more than a million users in just 5 days. To put this in perspective, it took Netflix 41 months, Facebook 10 months, and Instagram 2.5 months to reach the same number of users.

With its ability to generate human-like text, generative AI such as ChatGPT is currently helping build new search engines, create personalized therapy bots, explain complex algorithms, and even write college essays. Text-to-image programs such as Midjourney, DALL-E, and Stable Diffusion are changing the game for art, animation, gaming, and architecture. With this new type of AI, the creative process is set to get a whole lot faster, as artists and designers have a new collaborator to augment their existing tasks and speed up the ideation and creation phase. In fact, most of the images in this book were created by generative AI, so make sure to look closely.

But it doesn't stop there! Generative AI even has transformative capabilities in complex scientific disciplines such as computer science. Microsoft-owned GitHub Copilot, based on OpenAI's Codex model, supports developers with code suggestions and automates up to 40 percent of their work.

With all these innovative use cases we can see already popping up, optimists believe that generative AI is the foundation for the future of creativity and complex sciences alike. So the evolution of AI surely doesn't stop in the here and now. There are definitely some exciting times ahead of us!

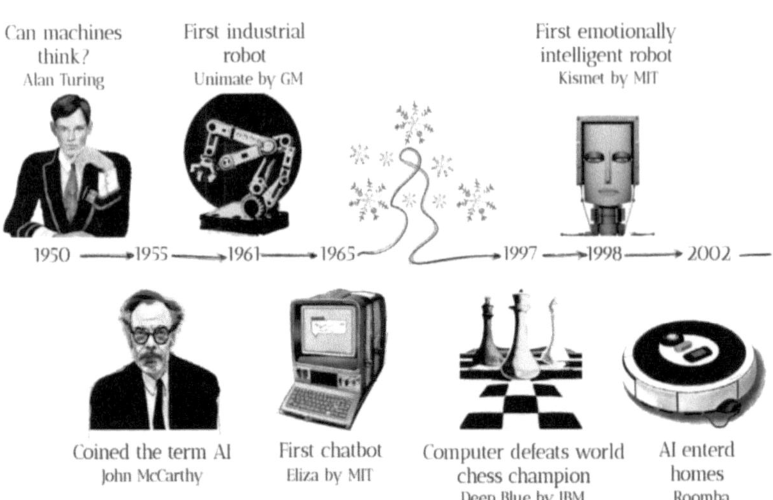

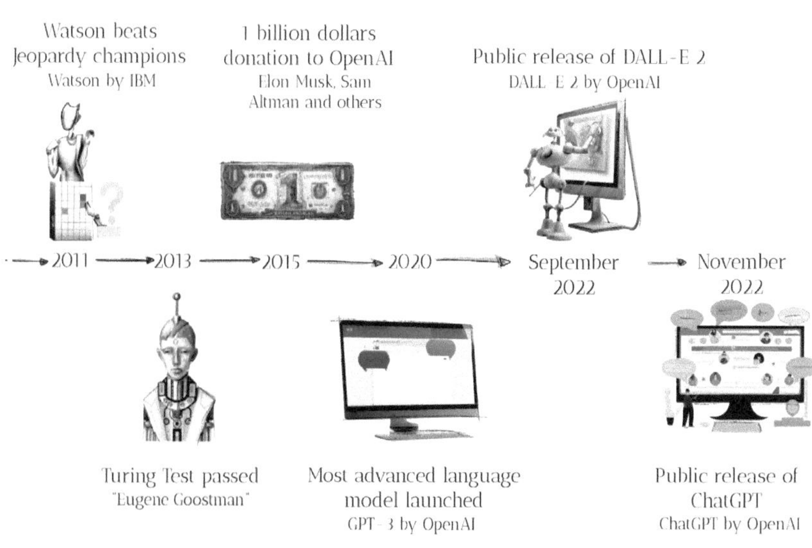

The Evolution of Artificial Intelligence: Milestones on our Way to the Intelligent Machine

BUZZWORD BINGO EXPLAINED: FROM MACHINE LEARNING TO GENERATIVE AI

Obviously, the basis of intelligence is—you guessed it—learning. Learning means we improve our performance in the future after we have observed and taken in some information about the world around us. This is no different for today's AI. In the world of AI, learning often means that we have a vast collection of input-output pairs, from which an underlying function is derived so the model can predict the output for new incoming input. Sound complicated?

Let's illustrate that with an easy example. Say we have a supercool collection of cute cat and dog pictures that show all different kinds of cats or dogs in them in all kinds of different situations. This is our input. As an output, we tell the model that these are either cats or dogs in the pictures. Now from this collection, we want to model to learn to recognize and distinguish cats and dogs. But not just those in our collection! This is no game of memory. That would be too easy. No; we want to feed the model a completely new cat image, and from this new input we want it to be able to predict that this is indeed a cat—and not our neighbor's tiny chihuahua.

You may wonder, why go through all this hassle? Collecting all these pictures and tagging all the cats and dogs in there so the program can learn. Why not directly tell the machine all the steps to take to come to solve a problem or come to a conclusion? Just like math lessons, couldn't we just simply let the program know all our math rules and functions so there is no more need for learning? Right . . . and wrong. This may work for simple tasks and problems. A lot of early AI research tried to teach the machine this way. And while they did have some success on smaller problems, they all failed miserably when it came to applying the models in the real world. And our world is messy, complex, and full of unknowns. So to be able to use AI for bigger and more complex problems, we need it to learn. Think about it. We simply cannot anticipate all situations the program will be in.

Consider a self-driving car. Now think about all cars on the road worldwide; the weather and road conditions; the cars' wear and tear; and other cars, people, or obstacles on the road. Quickly we must realize that it is simply impossible to prepare an AI system for all possible situations. So it needs to learn. Also, there may be changes with time. Consider a program designed to predict the stock market. Now a global pandemic comes along. It needs to be able to adapt when conditions change from boom to gloom to make good predictions. So it needs to learn. And most of all, sometimes we have no clue ourselves! Just consider our cat pictures. While it may be easy for us to say that these are all cats, even the best programmers might find it hard to boil that down into an algorithm—unless it is self-learning. So in short, for AI to become truly intelligent, it needs to be able to learn!

This brings us to the next point. How does AI learn? You may have come across many of the terms here: machine learning, supervised learning, unsupervised learning, reinforcement learning, deep learning. Basically these are all different ways of a machine, learning.

Machine learning is the broadest concept of them all. It basically refers to the idea that our algorithm is able to learn. Remember how we said that for very simple problems, we can tell a machine directly what to do. So it would look something like this: "if this"..."then do this." Clearly there is no learning from the computer's side. It is us telling it exactly what we know. Now consider a more complex task, such as teaching our machine to tell the difference between cats and dogs. As you can imagine, it would be extremely hard and complex to narrow this down to an if-then sequence. So we want the machine to learn. Or put differently, we use machine learning. Although it may sound complicated, the term basically refers to a set of approaches that all share the idea that a machine will learn from the data it is provided to improve its performance on a given task. That's it! That wasn't hard after all, right? And you have all seen them before, too! Familiar examples are the Netflix recommendation system, Snapchat filters, Google Maps, and Spotify-generated playlists. All use AI models based on machine learning!

Supervised, unsupervised, and reinforcement learning are all forms of machine learning. The only thing that differs among these types of learning is the way feedback is provided to the system.

Very intuitively, supervised learning means we give our algorithm all the feedback we can give. In short, learning is supervised. What does this look like? Well, we simply use so-called "labeled" data. This labeled data contains both input and output, meaning the output is already known. Think about our cat and dog images. Instead of just feeding cat and dog images into the program, we also tell it if there is a cat or a dog in each picture by labeling the images as either "cat" or "dog." So supervised learning is like having a teacher who shows you examples and tells you the correct answers. The more examples you see, the better you get at solving problems on your own. Once you get the logic, you receive new examples and solve them based on what your teacher taught you.

Clearly this labeling is time- and labor-intensive. So researchers tried to find ways around having experts painstakingly annotate data for supervised learning—and they have been successful! In 2022, a group of researchers were able to train an AI model called CheXzero to spot diseases on chest X-rays with medical reports that experts had written in natural language. And while you may think this hurts performance, it did not! In fact, the self-supervised model outperformed the supervised models with fully labeled data. This paves the way for self-supervised AI models that no longer need any data with explicit annotations and makes machine learning even faster!

Let's move on to unsupervised learning, which is, as the name implies, learning without explicit feedback. No supervision. This means that the program is not given any labeled data. Instead, the machine is left on its own to group the unsorted information by finding similarities, differences, and patterns in the data. It's like a detective trying to solve a mystery. It doesn't have all the clues up front, so it has to gather evidence and try to piece together what's going on.

Consider our cat and dog images again. This time we do not tell which image depicts a dog and which a cat. The idea of unsupervised learning is that by carefully examining each image, the machine can identify the clues that separate cats and dogs, such as the length of their tails, the presence of retractable claws, or the number of whiskers. After analyzing the evidence, the machine can group the images into categories, but it can't quite tell us if they are cats or dogs. Obviously this approach does not only apply to images of cats and dogs. In fact, this approach is often used in marketing, where marketers need to identify different customer segments. Through unsupervised learning, the AI can cluster customers together that share important features and are sufficiently dissimilar to other groups of customers.

Then there is reinforcement learning. You may have heard of this before. And you are right, reinforcement is a very common way we humans learn, too. When you think about reinforcement, think about rewards and punishments. We often use those in our day-to-day lives to reinforce positive behaviors in others while weakening negative ones. So we praise kids for eating their veggies while withholding the dessert if they don't. How does this relate to AI? Well, we can provide feedback to our machine in the exact same manner so it may learn the best behavior or actions. For example, we can reward it with two points if it wins a chess game and deduct two if it loses. Similarly, we can add points if it correctly identifies our cats and dogs in the images.

The goal for the program then is to maximize the rewards and minimize the punishments. The machine achieves this by deciding which action prior to the reinforcement (positive and negative) was most responsible for it. It will then show those actions more often that led to a reward and reduce those that led to a punishment. So if it was a kid at the dinner table, it would eat those veggies to gather more praise and eat even more to make sure it no longer misses out on that yummy dessert!

As you can imagine, the more data we feed our machine, the better for learning. So it is no coincidence that the rise of big data and advancements in computing power have led to even better ways of learning. This is where another form of machine learning, called deep learning, comes in. Deep learning is a type of artificial intelligence that's modeled after the way our brains work. Why is it called deep? Well, it's the scientists telling us that these models have multiple processing layers through which the data must pass. So our model of cats and dogs images would have several layers of abstraction.

Think of it like building a big network of brain cells, or neurons, that are trained to recognize patterns and make decisions. This network is fed massive amounts of data, and over time it learns to recognize connections and make predictions with a high degree of accuracy. It's like your brain: when you see a picture of a dog, it immediately recognizes it as a dog without you consciously thinking about it.

The deep learning network does something similar, but on a much larger scale.

However, one of the challenges with deep learning is that it can be difficult to understand why it made a particular decision. It's like the network has its own little "brain" it uses to make decisions, but it's not always easy for us to understand how it came to that conclusion. So, in a way, deep learning is like having a black box that can help you make decisions based on massive amounts of information, but it might not always be able to explain how it came to its conclusion. So deep learning represents a much more complex and larger-scale approach to machine learning. It requires huge amounts of data. But since we have lots of that today, we can benefit from highly accurate and intelligent machines!

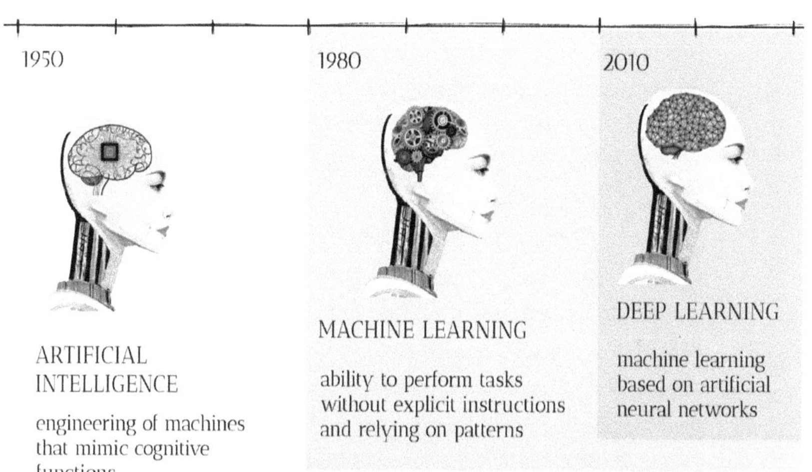

Artificial intelligence and types of machine learning

Which brings us to the final point: Generative AI. The current hype in the tech world, with ChatGPT, DALL-E, and Stable Diffusion just marking the tip of the iceberg! Deep learning algorithms are at the heart of generative AI, letting AI systems gobble up vast amounts of data and learn all sorts of interesting things. These clever algorithms then put their newfound knowledge to use by generating new and exciting data, such as text, images, and even audio! Hereby, a Generative Pretrained Transformer (GPT) is a type of language model that uses deep learning to create text that's almost like it was written by a human. These models are called "generative" because they can produce new text based on what they've learned, "pretrained" because they start by learning from a massive amount of text data, and "transformers" because they use a special type of neural network to process text.

Let's ask ChatGPT what generative AI is and what it can do:

> *Generative AI is a type of artificial intelligence that can create new and unique things from scratch, just like how an artist would paint a masterpiece or a musician would compose a hit song. It's like having a digital Picasso or Mozart at your fingertips!*
>
> *Let's take DALL-E, for example. It's a computer program that can generate images from text descriptions. Imagine you're sitting at home and you have this great idea for a painting, but you're not an artist yourself. With DALL-E, you can simply describe the painting you have in mind and the program will create it for you in the style of your favorite artist, let's say Picasso. You can tell DALL-E to "create an image of a woman with a guitar in the style of Picasso's cubism period" and it will generate an image that looks like it was painted by Picasso himself.*
>
> *It's not just limited to images, Generative AI can also be used to create new pieces of music, write poetry, or even compose a complete novel. The possibilities are endless.*

As ChatGPT so nicely outlines in its own words, generative AI creates something new and unique, unlike anything we've seen before. How is this different from prior machine learning models? Consider our example of cat and dog images again. We take a set of pictures of cats and dogs and train a model to recognize the common features of a cat or a dog. Then, when presented with a new picture, our classical machine learning model can identify if it contains a cat or not. With generative AI, we can go one step farther. Generative AI models can take inspiration from a set of images, such as pictures of cats and dogs, and create new images of cats and dogs that look similar and share common features but are not identical to the training examples. So the machine learning model does not only recognize but also creates new examples of the data.

Let's say you ask DALL-E to make a picture of an apple for you. The system has learned from millions of pictures and chiseled out patterns in them. For example, round objects such as apples and balls are placed in a "roundness" direction. And red things such as cherries and tomatoes are stored in a "redness" direction, and so on. So for our apple request, the AI already has information in store about what makes an apple look like an apple. This might include aspects such as that apples are fairly round, have a certain shade of red, and have a certain kind of texture.

Now when it's time to make a picture of an apple, it can use all of these directories to "imagine" a new picture that doesn't really exist but could. The AI will link all the directions it has collected and paints an image that has those overlapping qualities. In our case, it may use the "roundness" direction, the "redness" direction, and other directions to create a picture that looks like an apple. And the result? It may just feel like the AI is using its imagination to make a new picture just for you!

In the end, all AI models, whether generative or not, require data to learn and become truly intelligent. With the massive spike in digital data, AI now has more opportunities than ever to learn and grow! Just like a toddler who observes the world and receives feedback to learn what a dog or a cat is, AI today learns from the massive amounts of data we feed it. Unlike a toddler, AI does not need months to learn that. AI can process millions of images or texts in just a few minutes, making its learning abilities lightning fast. With access to more data, AI will only continue to evolve and continue to surprise us with the speed of its advancements.

AI OR NOT AI, THAT IS THE QUESTION

We talked a lot about learning and AI in the prior section. If these two are so tightly linked, you may wonder if rule-based algorithms are AI or not. Or do systems need to be self-learning to be AI? Unfortunately, there is no straightforward answer to this, and a lot of controversy still exists about what AI is exactly and what it isn't. In fact, a quick Google search with the question "What is Artificial Intelligence?" yields a staggering 1.28 billion results, and "Definition of Artificial Intelligence" generates almost 1 billion results.

At the broadest level, AI is often equated with algorithms. Algorithms are like recipes for computers. Just like how you need a recipe to make your favorite meal, computers need a set of instructions to perform tasks. Algorithms are step-by-step instructions that tell computers what to do, how to do it, and when to do it. But this broad definition of AI isn't very helpful because algorithms have been around for centuries and are used outside of AI. If we defined AI simply as the use of algorithms, it would include things like the instructions in a cookbook. That's not what we're talking about here.

On the other end of the spectrum, a strict way to define AI is as a technology that contains or entails human-like intelligence to realize complex goals. But that definition can also be problematic because many current applications of AI are still relatively narrow and not quite up to par with human intelligence when it comes to autonomously achieving complex goals in a wide range of environments. Defining AI like that would be like defining it out of existence.

So we turn to other definitions that focus on specific skills and tasks. For example, computer scientist Nils John Nilsson describes AI as a technology that "functions appropriately and with foresight in its environment." Others speak of AI's ability to perceive, pursue goals, initiate actions, and learn from feedback. These definitions are more helpful, but they still have limitations. For instance, a classic thermostat could also fit under these definitions. It can perceive (measure temperature), pursue goals (reach the programmed temperature), initiate actions (regulate temperature), and learn from feedback (stop once temperature is reached). But most of us wouldn't typically consider a thermostat AI.

A narrower definition many people seem to agree on is that AI refers to machines that can reason, learn, and perform actions that would normally require human intelligence. While this helps us understand the general idea, it leads to the next question: what is human intelligence? Despite years of research, we still don't have a complete understanding of how the human brain works and there's still a lot of debate and disagreement about what exactly human intelligence is, even among the experts. So using the term "intelligence" to define artificial *intelligence* is problematic, especially if we have no clear understanding of the concept itself.

Depending on whom you ask, you will get different answers to what AI is and isn't. As Russell and Novig point out in their seminal work on AI, definitions of AI differ based on two dimensions: some focus on the process, others on the resulting behavior; some use human intelligence as a reference point, others an ideal point of reference. So if we focus on acting like a human (resulting behavior focus), then yes, even rule-based algorithms or a simple calculator may produce results that seem intelligent. After all, being able to do arithmetic like a calculator can seem impressive, even if the calculator follows strict rules and did not learn any of the mathematical functions itself. However, if we focus on the idea that AI means thinking like a human (process focus), then no, a rule-based algorithm or a simple calculator would not be considered AI.

Today, many researchers agree that a focus on acting like a human and simply imitating human intelligence is not the way to make progress in the field of AI. Just as aeronautical engineers would not define their goal as "machines that fly so exactly like pigeons that they can fool even other pigeons," so do today's AI experts not focus on passing the Turing Test to fool someone into thinking they were interacting with a human while interacting with a machine. Instead, the focus of today's AI research is on systems that can "think humanly." So it's the process that counts. From this standpoint, a calculator is not AI. And calling it so today could be considered as "AI washing" by a lot of people.

The discussion, however, shows that AI is a multifaceted concept that changes over time. Existing definitions of AI can range from very narrow definitions that imply that AI does not exist yet, to very broad definitions that suggest that even a pocket calculator is AI.

So instead of seeing AI as a fixed concept with clearly defined methodologies, it is better to view it as a complex and diverse field focused on a certain time horizon. At the moment, this horizon is the understanding and simulation of all human intellectual skills, meaning general AI. But why focus all our attention on human-like intelligence? This has become the next big controversy in AI, and we will dive deeper into this in our next section.

AI IS INTELLIGENCE, "BUT NOT AS WE KNOW IT"

It is comparatively easy to make computers exhibit adult level performance on intelligence tests or playing checkers, and difficult or impossible to give them the skills of a one-year-old when it comes to perception and mobility.

Moravec (1988)

Why can a machine that can do lightning-fast complex calculations stumble when it comes to something as simple as holding a glass of water or tying a shoelace? Although these tasks might seem easy to us, they are actually incredibly complex when it comes to computation. For instance, when we tie our shoelaces, our brain's neural networks effortlessly process tons of information from various perceptual-motor systems without us even realizing it.

As biological creatures, our intelligence has evolved over billions of years to help us survive and thrive in the world. Our brain, a flesh-and-blood neural network, has undergone an optimization process that has resulted in an effective and efficient system for regulating essential biological functions and performing complex perceptive-motor and pattern-recognition tasks. These tasks include gathering food, fighting or flighting, mating, and even the practical skills we use in our daily lives, such as cooking and cleaning. They also include perceiving objects such as the words in this book, which we interpret much faster than the individual letters that make up those words or being able to quickly distinguish a domestic cat from a chihuahua.

All these tasks may seem very easy to us. After all, they don't even need our conscious awareness. Just consider how you can listen to a podcast while riding your bike or preparing your favorite pasta for dinner. Or how easily you can recognize your friend's face in a photograph without ever looking at individual components, such as the peculiarities of the eyes, ears, or nose.

Because these tasks seem relatively easy to us, we do not consider them very difficult. What does seem difficult to us, however, is multiplying two six-digit numbers or playing a game of chess. Paradoxically, what is easy for the ancient neural "technology" of our brains can be difficult for the modern, digital technology of computers and vice versa. This paradox, first identified by Hans Moravec in 1988, has come to be known as Moravec's Paradox.

While technology has clearly evolved since then, we can still observe hugely intelligent systems fail at seemingly trivial tasks. But consider how we assess the difficulty of these tasks. More often than not, we assess the complexity of a task in an anthropocentric way—or put differently, by the degree to which we humans can perform or master it. Riding a bike feels easy to us, so we consider it an easy task. And if an AI-controlled robot fails to show similar motor skills, we like to laugh at it. But when an AI system wins in the game of chess, a rather difficult task for us, we consider it highly intelligent.

We use our mastery of a task as a reference point to evaluate the level of intelligence of AI systems. But this rather subjective and human-centered approach can lead to a flawed understanding. Why? Well, because what may seem difficult for us humans—such as multiplying two six-digit numbers or mastering the game of chess—may not necessarily be computationally complex. And what may seem simple for us—such as riding a bike or tying our shoelaces—may not necessarily be computationally simple.

Why are computers so good at solving complex math problems, yet struggle with simple things such as recognizing a friend in a photograph? The answer lies in the fundamental differences between biological and digital intelligence. Our carbon-based brains and silicon-based computers are optimized for completely different kinds of tasks. Our basic biological and perceptual-motor abilities have been refined over millions of years. Our cognitive abilities and rational functions, however, are still relatively new in the grand scheme of evolution, making them—though hard to admit—rather limited in nature.

In short, while our brains are amazing, they also have limitations. For example, we can only consciously process so much information at once. In fact, research shows that our working memory is limited, with an estimated capacity of ten to fifty bits per second. This means that tasks such as reading or doing math require all our attention and take a lot of time. Indeed, mobile calculators can perform calculations that are millions of times more complex than what we can handle. And because our brains can't process lots of information at once, we're not great at "multitasking"—doing more than one cognitive task at a time. Don't believe it? Then try remembering a random sequence of information, such as 23ouobnw38JGi3, while doing the simple math below, and you'll see what we mean.

       7 x 13 =
       38 + 374 =
       196 - 52 =

Hard to do after all? Don't worry. Most of us struggle here. Our brains are capable of processing information quickly, but there is only so much that we can handle at one time. This means that when faced with a complex task, we may struggle to keep track of all the different pieces of information and make sense of it all.

Additionally, our acquired cognitive knowledge and skills, such as memory, tend to fade over time, much more so than perceptual-motor skills. This limited "retention" of information means that we easily forget substantial portions of what we have learned. While our brains can store vast amounts of information, we struggle to recall it when we need it. This is why we often forget things that we once knew or have trouble remembering names and faces. Think about it. Do you remember the full name of your high school crush? Surely you knew this piece of information at some point in time. But as the saying goes, if you don't use it, you lose it!

Unfortunately, that's not even all. In fact, our human cognitive processing is not only limited by its processing capacity but also prone to systematic distortions called cognitive biases. These biases occur unconsciously and feel natural and self-evident, leading to suboptimal decisions. For example, have you ever found yourself completely convinced that something is true, only to later realize that it was completely false? This happens because our brains have a tendency to believe what we want to believe, even if it goes against any objective evidence. In recent decades, researchers have uncovered many different cognitive biases that affect our judgments and our decision making. Ultimately, they result from the mismatch between evolutionarily rationalized heuristics and the current context or environment, leading to decisions that deviate from rationality and logic. But more on this in chapter 3!

The good thing of it all is that biology does a lot with very little energy. The human brain consumes less energy than a light bulb, while a supercomputer with comparable computational performance uses enough electricity to power an entire village. So our quick processing is good for something after all.

Now that we know what human brains are good and not so good at, what about AI? How is artificial intelligence different from ours? For starters, human intelligence is based on biological "wetware" made up of carbon, while artificial intelligence is silicon-based and digital. The "hardware" and "software" components of AI systems are independent of each other, whereas in biological systems, learning is bound to the individual system. So if you learn to ride a bike, you cannot automatically transfer this skill to your siblings or friends. This new skill is bound to your individual system. But if an AI system embedded in a robot learns to ride the bike, we can directly copy this new skill (embedded in the algorithm) to similar digital systems. Now all our other robots can ride the bike, although they individually may never have sat on a bike before.

Which leads us to the next point: learning. You may have heard that learning takes time. Yes, this is true for us humans. As humans, we have limited capacity for rapid structural expansion and immediate improvements. Just think about how long it took you to learn how to ride a bike or how many years you have spent in school learning how to do basic arithmetic. Learning in AI systems is different. Not only can any new skill be easily transferred from one system to the next, but also AI systems can easily be kept up to date, reconfigured, and expanded to meet changing requirements.

Plus, AI systems are lightning fast! In fact, in terms of response time, AI systems are many thousands of times faster than humans in reacting to simple stimuli. Why? Well, signals in AI systems can travel at nearly the speed of light, while in humans, the speed of nerve conduction is limited to 120 meters per second, which is quite slow compared to computers. In comparison, computers are true sprinters! But that's not even all. AI systems can also directly communicate with each other, allowing for efficient collaboration on integrated algorithms.

Humans cannot communicate with each other in such an efficient and direct manner. In fact, human communication is much slower and more complex and fuzzier than any machine communication, making it prone to mistakes and mutual misunderstandings. Just consider how often you have tried to tell someone an important piece of information that was received completely differently. AI systems are not prone to such miscommunications, as they can be directly connected to each other, ultimately making them intrinsic parts of the same system and algorithm.

Just think about two completely autonomous cars approaching a crossroad at roughly the same time. While we humans sometimes struggle to determine who can and should go first, this problem does not arise with AI systems, which have precise sensors, clear rules and can directly communicate if necessary. As humans, we have to communicate through language and gestures. So at the crossroads, you may wave at the other driver to signal she can go first. But she might interpret that as you saying, you will go first. In the end, both of you stand at the crossroad, no one is going, and then after waiting a bit both of you drive at once. Sound familiar? This is a typical example of human miscommunication. Unfortunately, this happens all the time and often even without us being aware of it.

Ultimately then, these inherent differences between human and artificial intelligence let AI perform tasks that even the most skilled human minds struggle with, such as playing unbeatable chess or detecting cancer with incredible accuracy. AI is like a super-advanced calculator capable of wonders. However, despite its impressive abilities, AI still has some limitations that can cause it to fall short of our expectations in certain situations. Indeed, as AI solely relies on prescribed rules or learned associations, it is vulnerable to unexpected twists and turns in the real world and can be easily fooled and confused by situations it has not seen before. This means that "corner cases"—situations slightly different from what the AI was programmed to expect—pose a challenge for AI.

Let's illustrate this point. You may remember how in 2016 someone used Tesla's Autopilot AI and caused a fatal accident. As later investigations revealed, the AI failed to brake when a truck crossed the road directly in front of the car. Although the AI was trained to recognize trucks, it could apparently only recognize them when they were moving in the direction of the car. So when suddenly a truck crossed the road, the AI ignored it just like a large street sign suspended over the road or any other stationary object. Unfortunately, this is just one example of a self-driving car that becomes confused by a scenario that a human driver could have handled with ease.

Another example from image recognition illustrates how AI sometimes seems to learn absurd rules that can then lead to problems in the real world. Specifically, researchers taught an AI to recognize a type of fish called tench in images. Everything seemed to work just fine until the researchers asked the AI to mark the pixels in the image that helped it identify a tench. Instead of selecting fins or scales, the AI highlighted parts of the image that showed human fingers. This sounds absurd at first, but there is a simple explanation: a tench is a trophy fish. As such, the data the AI was trained on included many pictures of a human posing with their trophy fish—and yes, holding it up with their hands so the fingers would always show.

These examples illustrate that AI systems simply recognize patterns in the data without truly understanding what the data represents. Here it is important to note that machine learning is primarily a tool for identifying patterns and associations in data. However, it reaches its limits when it comes to understanding the underlying dynamics or causes of those patterns, which may be extremely obvious to us.

Even the computer that mastered Go is simply identifying patterns in data. It doesn't have a clue that it's playing a game of Go or what would happen if half the board was suddenly pushed off the table. Sure, Alexa can use its fancy machine learning-powered voice recognition to quickly reserve a table for you at a restaurant, but does it really know what a restaurant is or what it means to eat a meal? If you asked it to book a table for two at 6:00 p.m. at a local Clinic, it would give it a shot—clueless about the real meaning behind your request.

All these shortcomings have one thing in common: they exist because today's AI lacks common sense and in particular an understanding of cause and effect. Common sense refers to the ability to understand the physical world and to use background knowledge to make predictions about it. This type of intelligence is critical for human reasoning and decision-making, as it allows us to make sense of the world around us and navigate it with ease. However, AI systems currently lack this ability. As highlighted by Yann LeCun, the director of AI at Meta, machines are still far from having "the essence of intelligence."

This shortcoming can cause AI systems to make incorrect or nonsensical decisions, because they lack the ability to understand the context in which they operate. For example, when Silicon Valley entrepreneur Kevin Lacker asked the language model ChatGPT "Which is heavier, a toaster or a pencil?" It answered, "A pencil is heavier than a toaster," while even a small child knows that the answer is the opposite. As humans we have mental models of objects such as toasters and pencils; we understand what they are and can picture their shape, size, and weight in our minds. But ChatGPT relies on statistical patterns found in its training data from the internet, and since there is not much discussion about the relative weights of toasters and pencils (at least not at the time the question was asked), it is unable to grasp this basic fact about the world.

As the "common" in the term already implies, common sense is something that we all possess. And as such, it is often overlooked as a rather simple ability. But it is far from that! Thanks to this set of universal axioms or rules, we are able to accomplish incredible things. For example, you don't have to make a conscious, complex calculation to know that a heavy rock should not be placed on a flimsy plastic table. Or if you read in an article "I stuck a pin in a carrot; when I pulled the pin out, it had a hole," you would know that the author was referring to the carrot and not the pin. Even the questions "Who is taller, Prince William or his baby son Prince George?" or "Can you make a salad out of a polyester shirt?" may seem trivial to you, but the answers require common sense. Clearly, if you want to make a salad but don't have any lettuce, you wouldn't waste your time trying to cut up a polyester shirt.

So common sense is everything but simple—and common only from a human vantage point! In fact, common sense is a complex and all-encompassing ability that includes not only social skills, such as recognizing and managing emotions, but also an innate understanding of physics and abstract concepts such as time, space, and events, allowing us to plan, estimate, and organize with ease.

Cause and effect are a major component of what we call common sense and a big part of our everyday life. It's how we make sense of the world around us. We know that if we drop a vase, it will shatter; if we drink coffee, we will feel more awake; and if we exercise regularly, we will be healthier. Today's AI can tell us that roosters crow when the sun rises, but it doesn't know why; it doesn't understand if the rooster crowing causes the sun to rise, or if the sun rising causes the rooster to crow. It's not designed to understand cause and effect in this way.

AI that can understand cause and effect could do so much more than what it can do today. It would be able to understand why certain things happen and not just that they happen. For example, if AI can understand that mosquitoes cause malaria, it can then reason about how to prevent mosquitoes from spreading malaria, and make real-world changes to make it happen. This kind of understanding is crucial for scientific thinking, and it's the foundation of science. It's the ability to form and test hypotheses about the effects of interventions in the world. Leading AI researchers have recognized this and have been working on developing AI that understands cause and effect. But it's still a tough challenge to solve. Making progress on this challenge will be key to creating the next generation of more sophisticated AI. But this will be extremely challenging, and it will take time.

Today, AI is a highly specialized tool created to solve specific tasks and problems (narrow AI, remember?). In contrast, common sense is more general and can't be defined by a set of rules. So think about today's AI systems in this way: they are like submarines, but they cannot swim like a fish in water. Submarines are highly specialized machines, designed for a specific task, but they lack the ability to navigate the open waters like a fish. Similarly, AI systems may excel at specific tasks, but they lack the general intelligence and common sense to understand the world around them and make decisions that are truly informed by context.

However, this doesn't mean that AI will stay that way. As we delve deeper into this realm, it's important to keep in mind that AI is not limited by the constraints of biological evolution, but rather the limits of physics and technology. And just like we can imagine a visitor from a distant planet having a unique form of intelligence, we can imagine AI having a structure and characteristics that are vastly different from our own. As AI continues to evolve and improve, it's likely that specific narrow AI capacities will match, overtake, and even transcend human cognitive abilities in the near future. And in the longer term, it may even become this AI buddy that understands the world as we do.

All of this might sound scary at first. But once we realize that artificial intelligence may look very different from our own cognitive abilities, we can find ways to use and collaborate better with AI. While AI may have the advantage in data processing and analysis, humans still have the upper hand in social-psychosocial interactions and adapting to unexpected circumstances for the time being. It is important to understand the similarities and differences between what artificial and human intelligence can and can't do well so we can capitalize on these unique strengths.

In the end, instead of defining AI as some technology showing human-like intelligence, we need to acknowledge that intelligence is a complex and multidimensional concept. Upon first look, using our human intelligence as a reference point sounds fairly straightforward. After all, we are the most intelligent on earth and beyond—and no one has ever told us otherwise! But if we look at nature, we may find that there are many other forms of intelligence that are considerably different from human cognitive abilities. And it may be hard to admit, but we humans are not always as smart as we would like to think. The truth is that our cognitive abilities have limitations too. These limitations stem from the fact that our brains are wired in specific ways to process information, which can sometimes lead to biases and misconceptions. So why focus the development of AI on human-like intelligence?

In other words: AI is intelligence, but different and not as we humans may know it. And it is important that we keep this in mind and do not unnecessarily restrict the development of AI (and its definition) to us as a reference.

CAN AI PAINT LIKE PICASSO? ON AI AND CREATIVITY

Creativity is one of the defining features of human beings. The capacity for genuine creativity, the kind of creativity that updates our understanding of the nature of being, that changes the way we understand what it is to be beautiful or good or true—that capacity is at the ground of what it is to be human.

Kelly (2019)

On January 10, 2023, Hollywood actor Ryan Reynolds posted a one-minute video ad for the mobile phone company Mint Mobile on YouTube. No big deal, right? Except it was written entirely by ChatGPT, the generative AI by OpenAI. In the new advertisement, the "Deadpool" actor claims to have asked the AI to create a Mint Mobile commercial in his voice, including a joke, a curse word, and mention of Mint's ongoing holiday promotion. Reynolds then reads what the AI produced:

"Hey, it's Ryan Reynolds here. First of all, let me just say Mint Mobile is the sh*t, but here's the thing: All the big wireless companies out there are ending their holiday promos, but not Mint Mobile. We're keeping the party going 'cause we're just that damn good. Give Mint Mobile a try and hey, as an added bonus, if you sign up now, you'll get to hear my voice every time you call customer service. Just kidding, that's not really a thing. Stay classy everyone."

The result is quite powerful and for sure raises some eyebrows in the creative services community. Reynolds describes the output as "mildly terrifying, but compelling." Just 24 hours after the video was posted, it already amassed 195,000 views. And, of course, people on YouTube had a lot to say about the new ad. One person commented, "I can't tell if Ryan actually wrote this or if the AI did, it's that good." Another viewer said, "It's kind of scary that ChatGPT can understand the kind of humor Ryan is known for and write something similar." The actor, who was in the commercial, also posted it on his Instagram and joked, "If this Mint Mobile ad is successful, I might have ChatGPT raise my kids too." Mint Mobile claims its new ad is the first to use generative AI in such a fashion.

There we have it. We live in a world where ad creatives are turning to generative AI like ChatGPT to generate ideas for brands, write rapid-fire briefs for clients, play around with ad copies, and come up with TikTok sketches. Generative AI is rapidly transforming the way we live and work. One of the most intriguing questions that has emerged from this new era of AI is whether it can be creative. What about one of the most important human abilities, true creativity? Can machines truly be capable of original, meaningful, and expressive acts of creation?

Just do a quick Google search for "AI painting" and you'll see a list of examples of AI-created masterpieces. Some of these paintings look like abstract art with random brushstrokes, but they're made by machines. This AI art is starting to be taken seriously. In October 2018, for example, the first-ever AI-generated portrait was sold at a Christie's auction in New York for a whopping $500,000. This price far exceeded the original estimated value of $10,000! In June 2022, Cosmopolitan made history when it became the first magazine to publish a cover designed entirely by AI. The team used the prompt "wide-angle shot from below of a female astronaut with an athletic feminine body walking with swagger toward camera on Mars in an infinite universe, synthwave digital art" to generate the image that was used for the cover.

Left: Portrait of Edmond Belamy, 2018, created by Generative Adversarial Network. Sold for $432,500 on October 25, 2018, at Christie's in New York. Right: World's first magazine cover created by DALL-E 2 from OpenAI.

So no question, AI can generate artwork, music, and literature that are impressive in terms of technical execution. But surely you will agree that true creativity goes beyond technical proficiency. So what exactly is creativity?

You may think of creativity as having a unique perspective and bringing new ideas to the table; the ability to generate new and original ideas, perspectives, or solutions to problems; a process that allows individuals to come up with something new, whether it be a new product, a new way of doing things, or a new form of art. So it's all about novelty, you may conclude. From this vantage point, we can categorize creativity into three different types: exploratory creativity, combinational creativity, and transformational creativity.

Exploratory creativity is about taking something that already exists and pushing its limits to discover new things. It's like being an explorer; you're setting out to discover something new, whether it's a new idea, a new approach, or a new way of looking at the world. It's like exploring the outer edges of what is possible while still following the rules.

For example, Bach's music is the result of a journey that baroque composers embarked on to explore tonality by weaving together different keys. His preludes and fugues push the boundaries of what is possible before breaking the genre open and entering the classical era of Mozart and Beethoven. Similarly, artists such as Pierre-Auguste Renoir and Camille Pissarro reconceived how we could visualize nature and the world around us, but it was Claude Monet who really pushed the boundaries, painting his water lilies over and over until his flecks of color dissolved into a new form of abstraction. Most of human creativity is exploration. This is the sort of creativity that AI excels at. It can perform many more calculations than the human brain and push a pattern or set of rules to the extremes.

Remember AlphaGo, which stunned the world by defeating world champion Go player Lee Sedol in a five-game match in 2016? What makes AlphaGo so remarkable is not just its ability to win at Go, but also the way it plays the game. AlphaGo has taught human experts that opening moves long thought to be ill-conceived can lead to victory. It plays in a style that experts describe as strange and alien. Unsurprisingly, many described the AI to be genuinely creative. However, others argue that this is not enough, as the game's rules are preformed, and the system can succeed only because it learns to play well within these boundaries. They argue that this is a very constrained form of creativity.

Another type of creativity is called combinational creativity. It's all about taking different things and putting them together in new and unique ways. It's like being a DJ; you're taking different songs and mixing them together to create a new track. For example, architect Zaha Hadid combined her knowledge of architecture with her love of the pure forms of the Russian painter Kasimir Malevich to create a unique style of curvaceous buildings.

This sort of creativity is also perfect for the world of AI; a coder can take an algorithm that plays the blues and combine it with the music of Boulez and create a strange hybrid composition that might just create a new world of sound. Of course, it could also be a dismal cacophony, so the coder needs to find two genres that can be fused algorithmically in an interesting way. Studies show that AI programs can compose music that sounds like it was created by human composers, imitating styles such as Bach's and combining them with other styles in innovative ways. But this is not the kind of creativity that is associated with innovative artists such as Schoenberg, who created a new way of thinking about music that spoke to the needs of his time.

This brings us to the third type of creativity: transformational creativity. This type of creativity is the most mysterious and elusive one. It describes those rare moments that completely change the game. Every art form has these gear shifts, like when Picasso introduced Cubism, Schoenberg introduced atonality, or Joyce introduced modernism. They are like phase changes, when water suddenly goes from a liquid to a gas. It's the type of creativity that is hard to program or replicate in a machine; it's about changing the rules of the game or dropping an assumption that previous generations had been working under. It's like a sudden catalyst that changes everything.

Can AI produce this kind of creativity? While a computer may not be able to initiate a transformative, game-changing phase shift on its own, it can be programmed to explore different possibilities and make unexpected connections, which could lead to a creative breakthrough. Additionally, by giving a computer the ability to behave irrationally, it can be programmed to explore new possibilities and make connections that may have been missed by humans. But even if this is so, would you call this creative?

If these three types of creativity were all there is to being creative, the output of today's AI systems may be considered creative to some extent. But some say there is more to creativity. Philosophers argue that the production of valuable novelty may be necessary for creativity, but it is not sufficient. Real creativity is an expression of intentional agency, meaning that creativity requires the capacity for conscious experience. It requires an agent who has a purpose and a sense of control over the outcome, a moral agent. Only when someone creates something intentionally, with a specific goal in mind and with the ability to make choices and decisions along the way, is it considered a creative act. Otherwise, it would only be considered as mimicking creativity. So while AI may be showing creative behaviors and outputs (resulting behavior focus), it lacks true creativity (process focus).

So creativity is not just about novelty, not just about producing something new and valuable. Consider a unique and intricate snowflake, a novel and tranquil pattern of dunes, or a distinctive and stunning array of colors at sunset. These natural phenomena may be aesthetically pleasing and new, but they are not considered creative. Why not? Because they are not the result of intentional agency. In other words: the water molecules, wind, and gases that create these natural phenomena are not agents who are responsible for what they bring about. For example, imagine you are snowboarding on a snowy day and your board tracks happen to trace out a pleasing pattern on the mountain. Although it is a new and aesthetically pleasing shape, it doesn't count as a creative act because it was a happy accident that you didn't intend.

Another crucial aspect of creativity is the ability to persuade others of the worth of our ideas. Albert Einstein is remembered as the "discoverer" of relativity not because he came up with equations that better describe the structure of space and time. In fact, others before him, such as George Fitzgerald, Hendrik Lorentz, and Henri Poincaré, had already developed these equations. But Einstein had an original and remarkable understanding of what the equations meant, and he could convey that understanding to others. For an AI to do something that is comparable to Einstein's creativity, it must be able to persuade others of the worth of its ideas at least as well as Einstein and other creative geniuses did.

In the end, when it comes to creativity it is important to note that different people may have different ways of thinking about it. What one person or generation may view as creative, others may see as crazy or ridiculous. Just think about Galileo Galilei and his conviction about the earth revolving around the sun. While we may think of him as a creative genius today, his ideas were deemed foolish and absurd at his time.

When it comes to whether AI can be creative, there is no agreed-upon answer to date. Sure, these programs can produce new and valuable things, but is that enough to qualify as true creativity? As humans, when we think of creativity, we often think of it as something that comes from a person with a unique perspective, who makes choices and decisions, and has control over the outcome. Does creativity require agency?

Can AI be creative even though it can't experience things as humans do? Opinions differ. Some say no, and find that AI can only be considered creative once it has consciousness. Until then, true creativity remains an exclusively human capacity. Others say the answer is yes, as consciousness is no prerequisite for creativity.

It's up to you to decide which side you take. Regardless of where you stand on the debate, one thing is certain: the outputs of these programs can be truly impressive. From painting in the style of Picasso, to creating a brilliant Go strategy, or composing music that rivals that of Beethoven, today's AI systems can produce things that are new, valuable, and often indistinguishable from human creations. However, these systems still largely rely on human prompts and are in no means autonomous creative agents. So if you are worried that AI will take over human creativity, remember AI is here to support and augment human creativity, not replace it. AI is a (creative) tool that enables human discovery, like the telescope that strengthened Galileo Galilei's belief in Copernicus's theory that earth, and all other planets, revolve around the sun.

CHAPTER 2

HEY, SIRI! ARE YOU HUMAN OR MACHINE?

As an old saying goes, "The more things change, the more they stay the same." In times when technology is changing at an ever-increasing pace, many of us may be tempted to look for that one constant in our lives. Researchers are no different. Trying to keep up with the technological pace, they look for fundamental and unchanging aspects to help us understand our relationships, both with each other, and any new technology. And guess what? In the face of the internet, social media, and even the AI revolution, the one constant moving at the slow pace of evolution is . . . our ancient brain!

Our brains have some pretty hard wiring that affects not only how we see the world, but also how we interpret the world around us. And if there is one thing that all of us remarkably unique human beings share, it is that we live and breathe together. And even—or especially—in times of smartphones and social media, research shows how important our social connections are for our well-being.

In short, we are social animals! As such, we have a lot of rules and norms that govern the way we interact with each other. For example, if someone gives you a flower, the principle of reciprocity would dictate you to return the favor somehow. So you might make a donation, sign a petition, or simply give the other person your biggest and brightest smile in return.

Today there is a new kind of social actor among us: AI—be it in the form of social robots, virtual assistants, or conversational interfaces. Of course, the more AI becomes part of our daily lives, the more we want and need to understand the rules and norms that govern this new kind of relationship.

So what if Siri or Alexa offered you some valuable advice? Would you return the favor? How about if an AI agent tells you its darkest secrets? Would you reciprocate? These questions might sound far-fetched or absurd, at least today. However, they are important to ask. And indeed, researchers have started asking them long before Siri and Alexa even came into existence. They looked at our computers for answers.

Clifford Nass, one of the pioneers in the field, conducted more than fifty experiments to observe how people interact with computers and to learn the fundamental rules that govern all of our relationships. And while he uncovered many social rules that dictate our interaction with other people, he also found that people mindlessly applied these rules to their interactions with computers and other interactive technologies. The result was the "Computers as Social Actors" (in short: CASA) paradigm, which countless follow-up studies replicated, even with more sophisticated technology than an old-school desktop computer. In the end, the idea was born that we treat technology as if it were a real person and show similar social reactions in these encounters.

So do we humans reveal intimate details of ourselves when a computer discloses seemingly intimate information? Yes, we do! Even if it is just mundane information, we feel obliged to give something in return.

Today, the idea that we mindlessly respond to any social cue, no matter if it comes from other people or a technology imitating them, has been rebutted. Countless studies have uncovered the many ways and instances in which our responses to technology differ markedly from those with our fellow human beings. However, the same rules and mechanisms that shape our human interactions can also be used to explain how we perceive and respond to AI. This understanding is crucial because how we perceive AI directly impacts our acceptance and trust of it. By exploring the nuances of our responses to technology and their connections to human perception, we can gain valuable insights into how our perception can be influenced, and actually is influenced, daily.

In what comes next, we show you when, why, and how your responses to AI may differ. And it all goes back to our brains. Or more precisely, our mind. Get ready for some mind-boggling insights!

DECODING THE MIND: UNLOCKING THE MYSTERIES OF MIND PERCEPTION

Imagine you need to prepare your family's New Year's feast. You ask a friend, a renowned cook, who recommends you a delicious meal everyone in the family will like. However, not everyone is so lucky to have a cook to ask.

So now imagine that you ask Siri, or another conversational interface in your home, for help. How do you think the recommendations will differ? And even more importantly, which one would you trust more and put all your cooking efforts in?

Today we know: even if the recommendations are exactly the same, who or what we believe to interact with determines our response! As a result, we may consider cooking the fancy recipe we receive from our human friend but dismiss the exact same dish from AI as weird and far out.

How we respond to the exact same outcome or recommendation depends on several factors. One important aspect, however, is how much mind we perceive in others. Which begs the question: who or what has a mind? It might seem obvious that you and those around you have one. But what about a fetus, a dog, or your Google assistant? How alike or different are AI and your fellow humans in this aspect? Does a social robot have more mind than a dog? Or a frog? How about a dead person or a newborn baby?

As you see, answers to these questions are not as straightforward. We may be tempted to ask others for self-reports or look at measures of brain activity to help us out here. But even then, how can you really know if they have a mind? In the end, the minds of others always remain inaccessible to us. This is why the answer to the question "Who or what has a mind?" is a matter of our subjective perception. And clearly, this perception can vary greatly from individual to individual and even challenge any objective evidence of mental capacities.

So it all boils down to this question: What exactly lets us perceive a mind? This question has long captivated scientists and researchers. It is not just limited to understanding the mental states of our fellow human beings but also extends to animals, robots, and even artificial intelligence.

Today, most agree that people tend to think about other minds in terms of two distinct dimensions: experience, the ability to sense and feel; and agency, the ability to plan and act. An entity can be high in both dimensions (e.g., you reading this book); low in experience and high in agency (e.g., God, Google); high in experience and low in agency (e.g., young kids, your cat or dog), or low in both (e.g., the deceased, inanimate objects).

This two-dimensional representation has emerged independently in several different research programs, including intuitive representations of personhood and the two fundamental dimensions of social evaluation. These findings demonstrate that when people attribute minds to others, it is in terms of their ability to "feel" and "do."

So agency refers to the perceived capacity to intend and to act (e.g., self-control, judgment, communication, thought, and memory). There are a number of cues that we use to infer agency in others, including the presence of movement that is flexible and goal-directed, as well as the ability to respond to environmental cues in a seemingly intentional way. Other cues include the ability to interact with the environment in a flexible and adaptive manner and the ability to exhibit self-initiated behavior. As a result, we are more likely to attribute minds to animals that move in seemingly goal-directed ways, or to robots that respond to our commands in seemingly intentional ways, than to inanimate objects that simply move in response to physical forces.

Research has also shown that we tend to attribute agency to entities that share certain characteristics with us, such as having a face, a body, or other features that are associated with being alive or having a mind. This is known as the "like-me" bias, and it is thought to be a result of our tendency to rely on our own mental states as a model for understanding the mental states of others. So yes, appearances can be deceiving when it comes to mind perception!

How much agency do you think a sociable robot has in comparison to a newborn baby, a dog, or a five-year-old kid? To answer these questions, researchers set up a survey and invited more than two thousand people in the United States to go through seventy-eight of such comparisons. For example, in one of these comparisons, participants had to rate whether a girl of five is more or less likely to be able to feel pain than a chimpanzee.

So where does our social robot stand in these comparisons? Well, it does fairly well in terms of agency! People perceive our robot to have more agency than a newborn baby, somewhere between a dog and a five-year-old girl. But this is where the good news ends. The agency of a human and even God was rated considerably higher. Thank God we are still in control! Or at least we think so.

Next to agency, perceptions of experience also play a decisive role in whether we perceive a mind in others. This refers to the perceived capacity for sensation and feelings (e.g., hunger, fear, and pleasure). It includes both positive and negative emotional experiences such as fear, pain, pleasure, desire, pride, joy, or embarrassment.

Humans experience a wide range of such emotions, from the pure joy of falling in love to the deep sorrow of loss. We express these emotions through verbal and nonverbal cues such as facial expressions and body language, which can facilitate communication and social connections. Imagine sensing the fear in someone's eyes, or the joy on their face, and understanding exactly what they might be feeling. Or consider seeing the wagging tail of a happy dog or the low growl of an angry one. This sense of emotional experience is what lets us perceive more mind in others, and it's what allows us to connect with them on a deeper level.

When it comes to such emotional experiences, it's easy to assume that they are limited to humans and animals. But the truth is, emotional experiences are not just limited to living beings, they can also be perceived in some nonliving entities such as robots and AI. Admittedly, robots and other technologies cannot experience emotions like we or animals can, but they can mimic them.

For example, some robots have been designed to mimic emotional expressions and behaviors, such as smiling or nodding, while many chatbots and conversational interfaces often work with emojis or expressions of emotion ("Oh, wow!") to feign feelings of surprise, joy, and such. Yet, coming back to our original questions, researchers of the aforementioned survey found that people consider the emotional experience of a robot as low as it can go. In fact, they attributed less emotional experience to a sociable robot than they did to a dead person, while a newborn baby, a dog, and fellow human beings all scored rather high on this dimension.

Dimensions of mind perception according to Gray, Gray & Wegner (2007)

Note that this snapshot was taken in 2007. Technology is getting more human-like every day. So the question is: how would you rate your domestic robot, such as an iRobot vacuum cleaner, or your digital AI assistant, such as Siri or Alexa, on these mind dimensions today?

As we delve deeper into the world of robots and AI, one question looms large: Why does it matter how much emotional experience and agency we attribute to these machines? The answer is simple yet profound: understanding the nuances of how much mind (i.e., emotional experience and agency) we attribute to technology and AI can help us understand our own interactions with them.

By recognizing that we attribute minds to others based on their capacity to "feel" and "do," we can better understand the complex and nuanced ways in which we perceive and interact with the world around us. And the implications of this understanding go far beyond surface-level interactions.

When we perceive a being as having more agency and emotional experience, we naturally begin to value them more. We want them to be happy and safe from harm. This perception also shapes our ideas of punishment and responsibility.

Think about it: our laws have long linked the idea of mind perception and morality. A person with low mental capacities is deemed less responsible for a moral transgression. For example, our laws would not punish a five-year-old in the same way as they would a twenty-five-year-old for stealing.

But it doesn't stop there. Our mind perception also affects how much we blame others in our everyday lives. Would you blame your colleague with a high agency for causing harm, or your dog with low(er) agency? The answer is clear. But how about an autonomous self-driving car that causes an accident? Or how about an AI system that didn't do so well in managing your financial investments? Would you hold the AI responsible for the outcome in the same way you would hold your human financial adviser accountable?

Our own research shows that this is not the case. Even if we experience the same bad investment results, we tend to place more blame on a human adviser compared to an AI system, and this usually results in greater dissatisfaction with the human adviser's service. As you can see, our mind perception can have dire consequences and our perceptions of the agency can matter greatly.

But the implications of mind perception go even farther. Not only do they affect how much responsibility we attribute to others, it also affects how much rights we afford them. The discussions on animal testing for medical treatments are a prime example for this. The more emotional experience (in particular capacity for pain) we attribute to these beings, the less we want to harm them. And since these perceptions are ultimately subjective and often independent of objective evidence, our opinions on this matter can also vary widely.

These perceptions also influence your decisions. Imagine being asked to harm one of two characters. Which would be more difficult for you to harm: a five-year-old girl or the robot "hitchBOT," which two professors lovingly developed in 2013 to hitchhike with people? Your answer reveals a deep connection between the idea of emotional experience and our ideas of rights and privileges for beings. And in case the answer wasn't already crystal clear: hitchBOT famously hitchhiked across Canada, Germany, and the Netherlands before it was stripped, decapitated and dumped on the side of the road during its journey in the United States.

Apparently, we do not feel (as) bad hurting or harming a character that (we think) does not feel anything when we do so. And while decapitating a bot might sound pretty brutal, consider the way you talk to your digital assistant—your Siri, Alexa, or Google assistant. Have you ever worried you might hurt their feelings, when talking to them harshly or impolitely?

If you are like most people, this is not any of your concerns.

Interestingly, research shows that this effect can also go the other way around. So any time we slip and do not behave like the virtuous person we would like to be, we dehumanize others so we do not have to feel so bad about ourselves. So we perceive less mind in AI when we are impolite or —as research has shown—attribute less mind to cows when we have eaten beef jerky. In short, stripping away the mind from others can be a very strategic move to convince ourselves that we are not so bad after all.

All of this aims to show that understanding our attributions of emotional experience and agency to technology and AI is crucial for understanding how we interact with these new interfaces. As you have seen, our mind perception affects our idea of the rights and responsibilities of AI. As appearances matter, we can use this knowledge to design technology and AI interfaces that can interact with humans in a more natural and beneficial way.

So next time you're wondering whether something has a mind, remember that it's not just a yes or no question. Instead, think about the two dimensions of experience and agency, and how they shape our perceptions and actions toward others, including AI.

MIND MATTERS: HOW OUR PERCEPTIONS SHAPE OUR INTERACTIONS WITH AI

Now that we know the dimensions through which we attribute more mind to Siri and the like, and also perceive them more as human, let's explore this question from another angle: what exactly makes a machine a machine? At its core, a machine is simply a device that can perform a specific task or set of tasks through the application of mechanical, electronic, or other forms of energy. This can range from the humble lever and gear to more complex machines, such as cars and smartphones. But when it comes to AI, things get a bit more interesting.

Remember: AI is the simulation of human intelligence in machines that are programmed to think and learn like humans. This can include tasks such as understanding natural language, recognizing images and speech, and making decisions. But where does AI differ from human intelligence? Well, the main distinction is that AI is based on algorithms and mathematical models, while human intelligence is based on the workings of the human brain. Additionally, AI is incapable of having emotions or consciousness, while human intelligence includes these elements.

Ultimately this lay theory we have about the inner workings of a machine (compared to humans), largely affects our beliefs and assumptions about it and when we will trust it (or not). So what are these assumptions we humans typically hold about algorithms and AI?

First, let's revisit the idea of emotional experience. As we believe AI systems to be these calculating machines, we tend not to consider them capable of experiencing emotions such as joy, anger, or sadness. But what happens when we start to see these machines as just that— machines? What happens when we believe they can't experience emotions as humans do? Researchers were wondering the same thing and asked people to play common economic games such as the Public Good game, the Ultimatum game, and the Dictator game. Some played these games with another human, others with a computer.

All of these games are essentially about trust and fairness. For example, in the Public Good game, players get to team up to build a common pool of resources. Each player can decide to either keep their resources to themselves or contribute to the common pool. The challenge is to convince others to contribute to the pool without going broke yourself.

In the Ultimatum game, two players get to split a pot of money between them. The catch is, Player 1 gets to propose the split and Player 2 gets to decide whether to accept or reject it. If Player 2 rejects the split, then no one gets any money. It's a tricky game of negotiating!

And in the Dictator game, one player gets to play dictator and decides how to split a pot of money. Unlike the Ultimatum game, there's no negotiation involved—the dictators get to make the decision all by themselves.

What do you think the researchers found? Did the dictators choose to share the wealth, or did they keep it all to themselves when they interacted with a computer instead of another human? The results were not surprising: people made more favorable decisions toward humans than they did toward machines. They allocated more money to a shared public good with humans, offered more money to humans in the Ultimatum game, and expected more money from machines before they were willing to forfeit an option where they kept everything in the Dictator game.

But why is this? It seems that when we believe machines don't have emotions, we don't feel guilty about exploiting them. We don't see them as beings that can feel pain or pleasure, so we don't have the same moral concerns when interacting with them.

But this lack of emotional experience does not only affect how we treat these systems. It also affects where we trust their advice. Imagine you're trying to decide between two different vacation options—one is a luxurious spa getaway, and the other is a backpacking adventure in the mountains. You're torn between the two, and you're not sure which one to choose. You turn to a travel agent for help. But this isn't just any travel agent; it's an AI-powered travel agent. You tell it what you're looking for and it provides you with a list of options. But something just doesn't feel right. You can't shake the feeling that the AI agent just doesn't understand what you're looking for and that it's not considering your emotional needs.

You're not alone feeling this way. Research suggests that in hedonic decisions, such as choosing a vacation, we tend to trust human recommenders more than AI-powered ones. This is because we believe that humans are better at assessing and understanding our emotional needs, whereas we see AI as more competent at providing logical, utilitarian advice.

This belief is rooted in our associations with how AI and humans process and evaluate information. We learn from a young age that we humans can perceive and connect with the world through our affective experiences, whereas we see AI as logical and lacking in emotional capabilities. This is reflected in idioms such as "thinking like a robot" and in popular culture, in movies such as Her, Ex Machina, and The Terminator, which reinforce these associations. This strengthens our belief that such unfeeling machines cannot understand our emotional needs.

But what about our beliefs regarding accuracy? Who do you think is more accurate when it comes to predicting the weather three days from today? A person, who claims to have a "feeling" about this, or an algorithm trained on past weather data? If you're like most people, you probably think that AI will excel at this task as it entails a lot of data processing, such as analyzing large sets of weather data and recognizing patterns. And you're right! These systems are great at tasks that require a high level of precision, such as predicting the weather, playing chess, or diagnosing medical conditions. So, based on the way these AI systems work, with all these data points and mathematical models, we are quick to assume they are also highly accurate in their predictions and recommendations.

Why do these beliefs about accuracy matter? They matter in trusting machines and AI over human judgment. In areas such as investment decisions or sports predictions, where there is a concrete, external standard of accuracy, we tend to feel more comfortable relying on algorithmic advice. But in personal taste, such as fashion advice or joke recommendations, we may prefer the advice of close friends over an algorithm.

Of course, the extent to which some decision domains may appear "algorithmically appropriate" to us also depends on the historical use of algorithms in this very context. For example, weather forecasts from meteorological models are widely accepted because we have seen them in use for decades, while the idea of fashion advice from algorithms is relatively new and may face greater resistance. However, as our experiences with AI and algorithms will change, so will our understanding of where we can trust its advice or not.

In the medical context, for example, we are still very much used to interacting with our trusted physicians. Although many studies have shown that statistical models often outperform doctors, doctors still prefer to rely on their own intuition instead of these models. In addition, doctors are seen as less professional and competent if they do rely on computerized decision aids. So while AI models can improve diagnoses and treatments in healthcare, we tend to resist medical AI and are not willing to pay as much for these systems. But why exactly do we resist medical AI?

This brings us to our next belief about machines and AI: We tend to see machines as rigid and inflexible. In contrast to humans, we think that algorithms and AI lack "cognitive flexibility." That is, they can't adapt their cognitive processes to new and unexpected conditions in the environment, which would require imagination and creativity. Instead, we assume that algorithms and AI can only operate in a standardized and repetitive fashion, based on their programming. Clearly, this assumption lets us believe that machines treat every case in the same way, without taking into account the unique characteristics of each individual.

As for our health, we often view our own circumstances and medical conditions as being more unique than those of others. We don't want to be reduced to a "mere number." We want to be seen as the unique individual that we are! As a result, when considering a diagnostic tool such as an automated dermatologist, we may worry that it won't take into account our unique skin characteristics to the same extent that a human dermatologist would. Or when considering a recommendation for surgery, we may believe that a computer won't take into account our unique symptoms in the same way a human doctor would. So especially when it comes to healthcare, we may be more resistant to using AI providers out of a concern that the unique aspects of our case will be neglected. And it all boils down to our idea that machines lack cognitive flexibility.

The idea that machines lack cognitive flexibility and instead operate in a very rigid manner has consequences beyond healthcare. Consider the following scenario: You're driving to work, and you decide to take a longer route than usual because of some traffic you saw. But when you get to work, you find out that the traffic wasn't as bad as it seemed, and you ended up getting there later than usual. Now, imagine the same scenario, but this time it was your traffic-sensitive GPS that made the mistake and advised you to take a different route. Chances are you'll be less likely to trust your GPS the next time you're stuck in traffic.

This is because the errors that we tolerate in humans become less tolerable when machines make them. In fact, research suggests that when machines and humans make (the same) mistakes, we tend to be more forgiving of the latter. After all, a human can just have a bad day and be fully up his game next time. The algorithm, however, is preprogrammed or programmed and as such fixed and consistent in its performance. Including its mistakes. A result of such beliefs: we expect the advice from AI to be perfect and show "algorithm aversion" when we see the machine make a mistake.

So while many of us believe that AI can outperform human judgment, such as our GPS knowing the quickest route, we more quickly lose confidence in AI when it errs. This is also because we assume that AI systems are unable to learn from mistakes and improve with practice as humans do.

However, this isn't really the case any longer. Modern AI systems can often learn from their mistakes and get better with feedback. If we show people that machines can learn, would you expect them to still quickly lose confidence and revert to human alternatives when mistakes are made? This is exactly what we also tried to find out in our research.

We set up an experiment with two recommendation systems. One was labeled as "self-learning AI," while the other was called a "rule-based algorithm." Participants were assigned to one system and had to make several investment decisions. Our systems were, of course, great. Until both made the same mistake and provided poor investment advice. But the experiment didn't end there. The participants had to make some more investment decisions, simply because we wanted to see how much they would still rely on our decision support system after seeing it err.

And what did we find? Our participants trusted the system more and rebuilt confidence faster after the mistake when we labeled it as a "self-learning AI" rather than a "rule-based algorithm." And we are not alone with such findings. Indeed, in a similar study researchers found that participants relied more on a learning algorithm than on a non-learning one. But even more interestingly, there was no difference in trust between a learning algorithm or a (learning) human adviser. This is good news because it means that highlighting an algorithm's ability to learn can help us overcome our algorithm aversion.

In the end, these findings show that we all have our own little "theory of machines" in our heads. It's these assumptions about what AI can and can't do that affect what we expect, how we behave, and if we trust in its advice. But here's the thing: these assumptions will continue to evolve and change depending on technological evolution and our experiences with technology. At the moment, most of us think that AI is great at boring and practical tasks that require data crunching and precision, while humans excel at creative and emotional tasks that require empathy and imagination. But as our experiences with AI change, so will our assumptions. So let's keep an open mind and embrace the potential of these amazing machines! Who knows? They might surprise us with their creative and empathic abilities any day soon.

Typical assumptions about what distinguishes humans from machines.

THE MIND MELD: WHEN WE PERCEIVE MINDS IN MACHINES

We've all been there—you're driving your car, and suddenly it starts lurching forward while braking. Suddenly your trusty vehicle seems to have a mind of its own. Or maybe you're playing a game against an AI opponent, and it makes a move that seems too clever and creative for a machine. These moments make us stop and wonder - do these machines have minds? Well, as you learned before, the answer is a bit more complicated than a simple yes or no. But what makes us perceive minds in machines? Recent research suggests that it's a combination of factors.

First, let's talk about unpredictability. When a machine behaves in a perfectly predictable way, it seems mindless. But when it starts acting up, such as Siri turning up the volume on your favorite song or your Italian Vespa scooter failing to start on a rainy day, our perception of its mind suddenly increases. This is because mental states—intentions, desires, and feelings—are the very states that best explain the behavior of independent entities. So we may be quick to think that Siri wants to cheer us up or Italian scooters must simply dislike bad weather. And there we have it: we have perceived a mind in the machine. Why? It all comes down to something called "causal uncertainty." Basically, when something behaves in a way that we can't easily understand or predict, our brains automatically start looking for a "mind" behind the behavior. This is why when your car starts acting up, it can feel like it has a mind of its own. Our brains are trying to make sense of the unpredictable behavior.

But unpredictability isn't the only thing that influences our perception of a machine's mind. Our own need for control also plays a role. When we feel like we don't have control over something, our brains start looking for something or someone that does have control. This is why people might start believing in a higher power or "agentic" beings when they're feeling lost or powerless. So if we feel like we don't have control over a situation, we may be more likely to attribute a mind to a machine to feel like we have a sense of understanding and control.

Next let's talk about similarity. We tend to see machines that resemble humans—or that we perceive to be similar to ourselves—as more mindful. On the other hand, machines that are different from us or that we dislike may be seen as less mindful. How quick we are to "see human" in nonhuman entities also depends on our personal need for social companionship. Just consider Tom Hanks in the movie Cast Away. Deserted on an island after a plane crash, a simple soccer ball with some stains on it is perfectly sufficient to see and interact with it like a human.

Similarly, we found that isolated people held longer conversations with their digital assistants during the coronavirus pandemic. This is because seeing mind in others also creates a sense of social connection. When we consider someone else's mental state, we start to see ourselves as more similar to them. This is why people who have a strong need to belong are more likely to see mind in others, and why feeling lonely can make us see mind in plants and machines.

But it's not just about how we perceive machines; it's also about how they are designed. Just consider the humanoid robot Pepper that smiles and waves at you at Pizza Hut and compare it to your autonomous vacuum cleaner at home. Who possesses more mind? The answer is clear. If a machine is designed to move and act in a way that is similar to humans, we are more likely to "see human" and attribute a mind to it. This is also called anthropomorphism— our tendency to imbue human-like characteristics to nonhuman objects. Anthropomorphism is why we may find ourselves having a greater emotional reaction to an AI system with a human-like appearance, one that converses with us in natural language, or one that moves at a human-like speed. Indeed, this aspect of technological design is so important that we have dedicated a section of this book to it!

But it's important to consider that similarity is not just about physical characteristics. Research has long shown that we tend to see entities—including other people—with similar beliefs as more mindful, while we see those with different beliefs as less mindful. To illustrate: people attribute more rationality and logical analysis to people with similar political beliefs than to those with different beliefs. Today, research finds very similar patterns and biases in our perception of machines. For example, if an AI system is programmed to make decisions that align with our own beliefs and values, we may see it as more mindful. So the way these systems are programmed to think and make decisions can also influence our perception of their mind.

In the end, whether or not machines have minds is a question that's still up for debate. But one thing is for sure: our perception of their minds plays a big role in how we interact with them. As technology and artificial agents become more advanced and integrated into our daily lives, it's important to consider how our perception of their minds influences our relationship with them. For example, if we perceive a machine to have a mind, we may be more likely to treat it with empathy and concern. This could have implications for how willing we are to replace it, how polite and courteous we are in our interactions, or how much we blame it for poor advice and recommendations. So next time you're talking to your car, or having a heated game against an AI opponent, remember it's not just the machine you're interacting with, it's also your own perception of its robomind!

PEEKING BEHIND THE CURTAIN: THE ART AND SCIENCE OF ANTHROPOMORPHIC AI DESIGN

As machines become more and more advanced and can perform tasks that once required human thought and judgment, an important psychological challenge emerges—will people trust these machines to replace human minds? An important line of research focuses on the role of anthropomorphism, the process of attributing human characteristics to nonhuman entities, in increasing people's trust in AI. An underlying idea of designers is to humanize AI to create trust and an emotional connection.

Think about it: when you're in rush-hour traffic, wouldn't you prefer a cabdriver who seems to be mindful and aware of his surroundings, over a driver who seems to be mindlessly engaging in an action without conscious awareness, foresight, and planning? Or when you're entrusting your health to a doctor, wouldn't you want one who seems thoughtful and analytical instead of just going through the motions? The same applies to technology. The more it seems to have human-like mental capacities, the more people may trust it to control its own actions and to perform its intended functions competently.

Researchers tested this idea with people's willingness to trust autonomous vehicles, or self-driving cars. They manipulated the ease with which a self-driving car, in their case approximated by a driving simulator, could be anthropomorphized by giving it a human name, gender, and a human voice. Their results showed that increasing anthropomorphism led to increased trust in the autonomous vehicle as people perceived it to be more mindful and capable of controlling its actions. So a little bit of anthropomorphism can go a long way in making our ride with AI more comfortable and enjoyable.

But it isn't only self-driving cars that have personalities of their own! Take a moment to look around you. You will start to see humanized objects everywhere! From the ads you see, to the logos and mascots brands use, to the design of their products. You will see that the M&Ms candy mascots look like little people, Kellogg's cereal products are marketed as if they're alive, the Amazon logo is smiling at you, and Lindt chocolate says "hello." Even government institutions use human-like features to promote healthy eating by giving fruits and vegetables human-like qualities. The truth is, designers put a lot of thought and care into making these objects be as "human" as needed to elicit the desired response from the user.

But what exactly goes into creating seemingly human-like systems? Let's take a deeper look into the mind of AI designers and see how they blur the lines between human and non-human!

The key to success is the application of "anthropomorphic features," which imitate human-like characteristics in nonhuman technological agents to improve our connections with them. These features can be divided into three broad categories: visual and auditory features, which can be directly perceived through our senses; and mental features, which require a more cognitively complex inference process. Visual and auditory features include things such as a robot's appearance and voice, which can lead to the perception of biological gender and associated behavioral, cultural, or psychological traits. Mental features include things such as context understanding and dialog ability, which can be conveyed through speech output or text on a screen.

Let's start with visual features. Imagine a virtual assistant that is designed with an avatar-based interface featuring a human-like face or body. As you talk to it, you can see it smiling and nodding along with your conversation. This may seem like a small detail, but research has shown that having a virtual agent with a human-like appearance can significantly improve the bond between the human and the virtual agent, especially in social interactions. We naturally feel more comfortable and have a greater sense of trust and connection with the technology.

Why is this important? Consider the growing need for social support and companionship in elderly care. Here, robotic pets, designed with human-like features such as eyes, ears, and a mouth, have emerged as a promising solution to this need. These technological companions are equipped with sensors and AI, making them capable of interacting with elderly individuals in meaningful ways. They can help to alleviate loneliness and improve the mental well-being of the elderly. But clearly it doesn't stop there. Social robots, which are designed to look and act like humans, are increasingly used in healthcare settings such as hospitals and nursing homes to provide companionship and support to patients. By designing technology with human-like visual features, interacting with AI feels like having a friend or colleague right there with you, helping you out with whatever you need.

Visual features are not everything, of course. AI designers often work with auditory features as well. Imagine a voice recognition software that can understand and respond to your every word. It's not just about being able to control your technology with your voice, but also about the way the software speaks to you. The tone, inflection, and even gender of the voice can convey a sense of trust, understanding, and even empathy.

For physically or visually impaired people, auditory features can greatly improve the usefulness and ease of use of the technology, and make it feel like it truly understands and cares about their needs. A prime example of humanized auditory technology are today's digital voice assistants, such as Apple's Siri or Amazon's Alexa, which are designed to interact with users in a conversational manner, using a natural language interface. Similarly, some virtual personal health assistants use a human-like voice to guide patients through medical procedures, helping to calm and comfort them in potentially stressful situations.

Finally, a word about the role of mental features in the humanization of machines. Imagine a virtual agent that can assess and respond to your emotions. It can read your facial expressions, your tone of voice, and even your body language. Sound far-fetched? Big Tech has long developed AI models to learn about your moods and emotions. Affectiva can read your emotions from your face, Beyond Verbal uses your tone of voice, and Facebook looks at your language in status updates or comments. Once AI knows how you feel, it can respond to you with empathy, understanding, and even a sense of humor. It's not just about the technology being able to perform its tasks, but also about it being able to truly connect with you on a human level. One way we humans do this is by mirroring the other person. And AI is currently taught to do the same. As you can imagine, this is the most complex and challenging category of anthropomorphic features. But it can be the most powerful and transformative.

And at last, AI designers have to consider all three categories together to make the experience consistent for the user. When using multiple anthropomorphic features, it's important to make sure that they all align and convey the same gender or personality. For example, if the appearance of an AI system suggests a certain gender, the voice should also suggest the same gender. Providing a coherent picture to the end user can be tricky and requires a lot of thought and care. But if done successfully, anthropomorphic features can bring a human touch to the way we interact with machines. It can improve the user experience and increase customer acceptance and adoption of robots in service settings. It also has been found to improve our evaluations of robots' social cognition such as a sense of warmth. Additionally, anthropomorphism has been shown to increase our engagement, satisfaction, and ultimately even our willingness to pay for services offered.

As a result of these positive findings, technology companies are constantly working to make their products more human-like by incorporating features such as voice synthesizers, emotional expressives, or imitating the users' unique language styles. This is done in the hope of providing a greater human touch to the user experience and to improve customer satisfaction. And indeed, research shows that in automated user assistance systems, anthropomorphism can lead to a more personalized experience for customers and improve their overall satisfaction. Similarly, anthropomorphizing chatbot interactions can lead to closer ties with customers and increase loyalty.

In short, we like what is similar to us. Following the logic, we also tested how users would react if a chatbot uses a language style that matches their own. And indeed, our participants reacted very positively to the chatbot that communicated in a way they did. Not only did the participants process the information more quickly, they also felt more rapport with the chatbot and even were more inclined to follow its advice! So without being consciously aware about it, we all tend to react very positively to technology that is more like us, be it through visual cues, auditory features, or mental cues.

It's easy to get caught up in the excitement of humanizing AI and the potential benefits it brings. We imagine talking to our virtual assistants and having them sound just like our best friends, or interacting with customer service robots that act and behave just like humans. But before we jump to conclusions and assume that more human-like features always lead to better outcomes, it's important to remember that there are other factors in the design of technology.

Sure, anthropomorphism can greatly improve the user experience by making technology more relatable and easier to interact with. But sometimes a more straightforward and less human-like approach might be more effective. It's like a chef adding the perfect pinch of salt to bring out the flavors in a dish. In the same way, the key to designing technology with anthropomorphic features is to understand when and how many human-like features are needed to achieve the optimal user experience, rather than simply adding human-like features for the sake of it.

Consider the following example. In our own research, we created two chatbots: one that was programmed to be social and human-like, using linguistic expressions such as "hmms" and "ahas" to make it seem like a real person, and another that was functional and machine-like, sticking to the script without those typical social expressions. Essentially, we wanted to find out if our participants would be more concerned about how well they present themselves and how well they are received when interacting with humanized technology. That's precisely what we typically do when interacting with other people.

And our results were surprising! People who interacted with the social chatbot were more concerned about how they came across during the conversation. They even answered sensitive questions in a more socially desirable way, compared to when they talked to the machine-like chatbot. For example, we asked participants about the number of sexual partners they had had. Men boasted of having many sexual partners, while women reported having few when they talked to the social chatbot; these results flipped for those who talked to the machine-like chatbot: women reported having had a few more sexual partners, and men reported having had fewer. And that's just one example. It vividly demonstrates that our behavior becomes increasingly social as technology is designed to be more human-like. In our study, participants gave more socially desirable answers when speaking with the humanized chatbot. Women were likely more concerned about having had too many sexual partners, while men were worried about having too few. It seems our participants wanted to leave a good impression on our humanized chatbots, just as they would with other people. With our functional chatbot, however, participants were less concerned about how their answers would be received and even rated the same sensitive questions as less sensitive!

In short, as our example shows, sometimes it's best to let machines be machines instead of making them indistinguishable from us. We need to think about the kind of user behavior we want to promote. Do we want people to interact socially with technology or do we want to take the social aspect out of the equation?

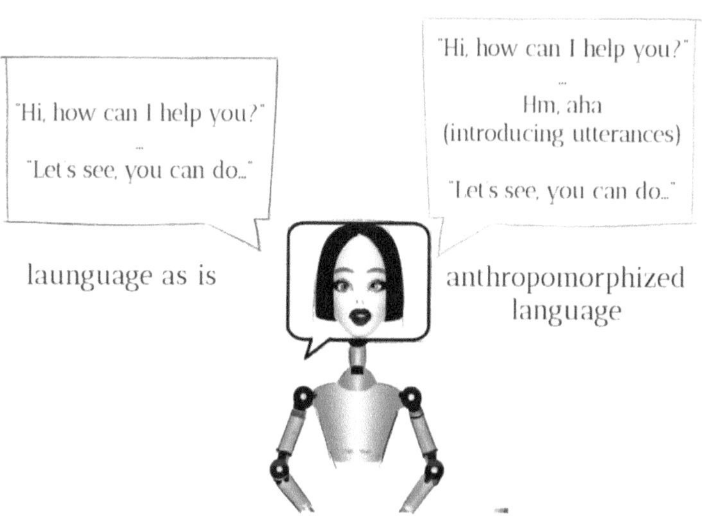

Anthropomorphizing AI communication.

This brings us to the next point: The degree of humanization should depend on the specific task and situation. Imagine you're trying to navigate through a complicated website. In this case, you probably want a clear and straightforward user interface that allows you to quickly find the information you're looking for. An overly human-like interface, where, for example, you have to engage in lengthy conversations with a chatbot, would be more frustrating than helpful. However, when you have a problem and need customer support, a more human-like approach might be more effective in creating a personalized experience. Ultimately, it's all about finding the right balance of human-like features depending on the task at hand.

Clearly then, it's also important to consider the context of the interaction. For example, in situations where people's emotions can run high, such as financial decisions, a more straightforward and less human-like approach might be more effective. When faced with a more human-like machine, people may react more emotionally and make gut decisions. In such cases, reducing the machine's human-like qualities can lead to more rational decision-making by the users. Another situation is where we might fear social judgments from others. Think about it: when we interact with people, we're always worried about being judged and what others will think of us. And guess what? This behavior also extends to our interactions with technology, especially when it is designed to be more social and human-like. Picture a person struggling with incontinence; openly discussing this issue could be difficult. Our own research shows that less human-like chatbots can help people talk about sensitive topics. In fact, the very same questions are perceived as less sensitive when asked by a non-human bot! In the end, a very functional chatbot can help people open up more easily—and be more honest about their needs or fears.

But humanization of technology does not only affect our behavior and responses. It also affects our expectations.

This is another reason why humanization may not always be desirable: it can create unrealistic expectations and demands on machines. When machines look and act like humans, people may expect them to have the same level of intelligence, empathy, and social skills as real humans. However, machines are still limited in their ability to understand and respond to human emotions, social cues, and contexts. This can lead to frustration and disappointment when machines fail to meet these unrealistic expectations. The chatbots of recent years are the best example of this.

Even more so: if a machine tries to look and act like a human but it's not quite there yet and doesn't match our expectations, it can make us feel uncomfortable. This is the "uncanny valley" effect. Basically, the term is used to describe the discomfort or eeriness that can arise when robots or other human-like machines look and act almost, but not quite, like real humans. It was first proposed by roboticist Masahiro Mori in 1970. Mori theorized that as robots become more human-like, people's sense of familiarity and comfort with them increases. However, as the robots approach a level of human-likeness that is almost, but not quite, realistic, people's sense of familiarity and comfort drops sharply, resulting in feelings of eeriness and unease.

The uncanny valley effect can be seen in a variety of examples in our everyday lives. For example, have you seen the animated movie The Polar Express? The movie was released in 2004, directed by Robert Zemeckis, and starred Tom Hanks. It was based on motion capture technology to create the animated characters, including a character voiced by Tom Hanks. While the technology used to create the movie was cutting-edge at the time, many viewers and critics felt that the characters in the movie looked and moved unnaturally. The characters' facial expressions and movements, especially their eyes and mouth movements, were perceived as robotic and not quite realistic enough, which led to some viewers feeling discomfort or unease while watching the movie. This effect was particularly noticeable in scenes where the characters were in close-up or interacting with other characters. So if you haven't seen the movie but want to experience an uncanny valley effect firsthand, that's the way to go!

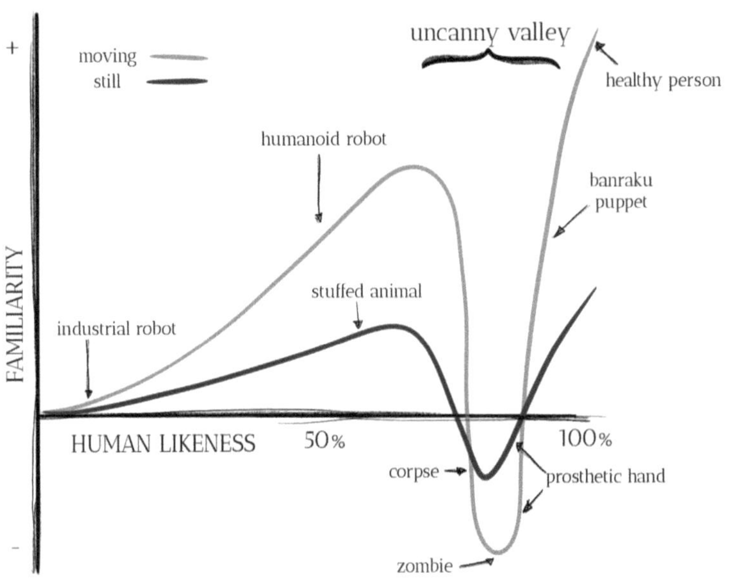

The Uncanny Valley (Mori 1970)

Other examples you may have experienced are customer service chatbots that are programmed to sound and act like a human. At first these chatbots might seem helpful and efficient. But as the conversation goes on, you might start to notice that the chatbot's responses are a little too robotic or stilted. Again, this can cause feelings of discomfort and mistrust. Similarly, a humanoid service robot that is designed to look and move almost like a human, but not quite, can also give people the creeps.

Indeed, researchers show that humanoid service robots that make you feel eerie can lead to compensatory consumption! So when encountering an „almost human" service robot, customers at a restaurant ate more, especially unhealthy food; customers in a store purchased more status products; and customers in a hotel setting tried to cope with their feelings of discomfort by seeking out other people close by. These findings show that humanoid service robots that look almost but not quite human may elicit feelings of discomfort, fear, or even revulsion in some people. This can make it difficult for people to interact with such machines and can undermine their potential benefits.

There are a few different theories about why this happens. Some people think the uncanny valley effect arises because machines that look too human can remind us of our own mortality, which can be scary. Others think it's because we worry that robots might take over our jobs or even our world someday. Still others suggest that it is a result of the mismatch between our expectations of how human-like technology should behave, and the reality of how it actually behaves. And then there are some scientists who think this is because we have an instinct to be wary of things that look almost human, but not quite. Whatever the reasons may be, the uncanny valley effect shows that even though robots and AI systems can be really helpful and cool, sometimes it's better if they don't look or act too much like us.

In the end, it is important to remember that modern technologies are no longer just mere tools, but play an increasingly important role in our daily lives and even take on social tasks. As such, it is crucial to design technology in a way that not only meets practical needs, but also appeals to us on a psychological level. In short: we need to consider the psychological dimensions of technological design. Using anthropomorphic features is a balancing act: on the one hand, we want to encourage a natural interaction with technology; on the other hand, we need to take into account users' expectations and needs. The key lies in understanding that it's not about adding human-like features for their own sake; rather, we need to discern when and how many human-like features make sense to ultimately create an optimal user experience and elicit the desired response from users. In the end, this is a process that doesn't happen casually but requires a deep understanding of human perception and cognition.

Now you are an expert on anthropomorphism and its role in human-computer interaction. With this newfound knowledge, you can take a fresh look at the many technologies around you and uncover the hidden motivations of the designers. Pay attention to technology design in your everyday life. Are there any human-like features present? If so, which ones? Do they feel natural and consistent, or do they seem out of place? Did the designers go overboard and create unrealistic expectations or an eerie vibe? Try to understand why the designers have included these features and whether or not they were successful in achieving their desired goal. And remember: finding the right balance of human-like features is key to creating a fantastic user experience. So keep an eye out for those sweet spots where technology and humanity meet!

CHAPTER 3

THE PERKS OF TEAMING UP WITH AI

It's a debate that's as old as time: will AI take over the world and leave us humans in the dust? The answer isn't so cut and dry. Although they may have similar qualities and capabilities, AI and human beings are far from the same. Sure, AI will definitely change the way we work and live, and some jobs will certainly become obsolete. However, the aim of AI is not to replace us but to empower us, creating new job opportunities. This is essential, and only the ones who realize this will be able to truly experience the perks of teaming up with AI.

The question of whether AI will replace human workers assumes that AI and humans have the same qualities and abilities. Let's remember that AI and humans are distinctively different, each with its own unique talents and with decidedly different types of intelligence. AI-based machines may be lightning-quick, pinpoint-accurate, and more rational (or maybe not? we'll get to this later). AI can sniff out useful information and make sure trends stay on track. Best of all, it never gets exhausted, like us humans; as long as it's fed with data, it'll keep on working! However, these machines don't have the intuition, emotions, creativity, or cultural savvy that humans have, and it's these aspects that make us so extraordinary.

It's clear that both humans and AI can be a powerful duo, each bringing their own talents to the table to create something greater than the sum of their parts! Research has proven that the most significant performance improvements happen when humans and AI work together, not when AI replaces humans. For example, think of the game of chess. You probably knew that AI today can beat any human grandmaster. But did you know that the combination of a human chess player and AI can beat not only any human but also any machine? It's the same in other fields too; physicians collaborating with AI have been shown to have better accuracy in diagnosing skin cancer than either AI or physicians alone. AI can analyze large amounts of medical data and identify patterns that may not be obvious to humans. However, a doctor's expertise and experience in diagnosis can provide important context and insight that can improve the accuracy of the AI's recommendations. In fact, recent studies have shown that doctors using AI are able to catch breast cancer more frequently than either doctors or AI alone. And that same AI is even producing more accurate results when in the hands of a radiologist compared to when it's working solo.

To truly unlock the benefits of working with AI, we need to shift our thinking from seeing it as a threat to our abilities to viewing it as a collaborator that can help us become even better. Just like the legendary criminal duo Bonnie and Clyde, human-AI collaboration involves combining different skills and abilities to achieve a common goal. Instead of robbing banks and plotting against the law, our modern-day Bonnie and Clyde use their combined talents to develop innovative solutions to some of the world's most challenging problems. While AI excels at tasks such as crunching large amounts of data and solving puzzles, humans bring unique strengths such as creativity, empathy, and common sense to the table. Of course, this human-AI collaboration requires teamwork and coordination, just like Bonnie and Clyde had to work together and communicate to carry out their crimes. It may also involve taking calculated risks in terms of trying new technologies or approaches to problem-solving to achieve greater rewards. But unlike Bonnie and Clyde, these successes don't come at the expense of others. Instead, human-AI collaboration can have a positive impact on society and help us achieve goals. We hope that after reading this chapter, you will view AI as your partner rather than your enemy.

PRECISION PERFECTION: ON OUTPLAYING THE EFFORT-ACCURACY TRADE-OFF

The modern world is a dizzying array of sources of information, with news feeds, feeds from social media, data from scientific and business sources, videos, music, and more. Today, in just 60 seconds, more than 3 million Facebook posts appear, 500 hours of YouTube videos are uploaded, and 150,000 emails are sent. With the digital age of the twenty-first century, you can stay up to date on all the latest news, no matter where you are! You can watch a "breaking news" story on TV while your smartphone buzzes with notifications about the latest tweets from your favorite political candidate. You can read magazine articles and check out posts on Instagram, all within a few inches of your fingertips. In addition, you can find out anything you want to know in seconds, from why dogs bark to the best yoga retreats in the world. And don't forget to read the thousands of reviews about the shoes you are about to buy! Want to listen to a song? Sure—here are thirty million songs to choose from.

Having so much information at your fingertips is awesome, but you know how they say, "too much of a good thing can be a bad thing"? Well, that's definitely true about information. This is called "information overload," and it can be overwhelming. We experience information overload when we try to make a decision or make up our minds about a topic but there is too much information available. The sheer quantity, speed, and diversity of information have outpaced what any individual can process, making it difficult to determine what is relevant or important. As a result, we often are overwhelmed, finding it difficult to understand an issue or make good decisions.

For example, scientists are publishing millions of academic articles every year. This means there's a wealth of information that can help us better understand an issue. But reading all the articles would, of course, take forever. The coronavirus pandemic is a prime example. In the first six months of 2020, the number of articles published about it went from zero to an incredible twenty-eight thousand. In mid-May, nearly three thousand papers were published in a single week! It would be impossible for a researcher to read this many papers and still manage to do their own research. The situation wasn't any better for citizens trying to figure out what to do to protect themselves and their families. With such a vast amount of information available, it was difficult to determine which sources were reliable and which recommendations were backed by scientific evidence. In addition, the rapidly changing nature of the pandemic meant that new information was being published almost daily, making it even harder to keep up with the latest developments. As a result, many people found themselves overwhelmed by the sheer amount of information available and unsure of how to interpret it.

Given that we only have limited cognitive resources to process information, we usually face a trade-off between accuracy and effort when making decisions. Put simply, you can either spend a lot of time and effort sorting through all available information, carefully analyzing and processing it, to make a more accurate decision. Or you can make decisions quickly to save time and effort, but this often comes at the cost of accuracy. More often than not, we opt for the latter strategy, as our time and energy are limited resources that we'd rather save them for the most important aspects of our lives (at least this is what we tell ourselves while scrolling through our social media feeds for hours). During the pandemic this meant that many people simply gave up on keeping track of the latest developments, choosing instead to rely on the general recommendations of their local authorities, trusted healthcare providers, or favorite social media influencers. All of these sources help us make faster decisions—often, however, at the expense of accuracy.

AI can help us overcome this effort-accuracy trade-off. Not only does AI help us make decisions more quickly to save time and effort, it also increases our accuracy if designed carefully. In fact, we are sure AI already helps you deal with information overload day to day, even if you may not even be aware of it. For example, have you ever used a streaming service such as Netflix or Spotify? These companies use AI and "collaborative filtering" to recommend shows and songs based on your viewing and listening history, as well as the histories of other users who have tastes similar to yours. For example, if you love action movies, Netflix might suggest some action flicks that other action movie fans loved. This way, you're more likely to find movies that you'll enjoy watching. In short: AI-powered recommendation systems can provide personalized recommendations to help you quickly find the information or products and services that are most relevant to you.

Another way AI helps us deal with information overload is with summarization. For instance, have you ever used a virtual assistant such as Siri or Alexa? These handy helpers use natural language processing (NLP) to understand your commands and provide appropriate responses. It's a way for computers to understand and analyze human language and can be used to automatically summarize long articles or documents into shorter, easier-to-digest versions. This is great for busy bees who don't have time to read lengthy articles but still want to stay informed about their field. Another example is the generative AI ChatGPT. The AI system can be used to automatically generate concise summaries of long conversations or chat logs, helping users to quickly understand the main points and avoid being overwhelmed by a large volume of text.

But AI isn't just about recommendations and summaries; it can also help with organization and curation. For example, if you've ever used a search engine such as Google, you've probably experienced the power of AI-powered search firsthand. The algorithms used by these platforms use AI to understand your search query and to classify and tag large volumes of data, making it easier for us to find what we're looking for. In short, these AI systems can help reduce information overload by providing concise, relevant information to individuals.

However, with great power comes great responsibility! As these AI systems increasingly shape our everyday lives and the way we see the world, it is of course critical that such systems are carefully designed and implemented to ensure that they are providing accurate and reliable information (more on this later). Once they are, and you understand how they shape your world, they can be the best secretary, news curator, or shopping assistant you have ever known! So next time you're feeling overwhelmed by the deluge of information and choices, remember that AI has your back! It's using all kinds of clever tricks to help us sift through the clutter and find that needle in the haystack we did not know we were looking for all along.

SMARTER DECISION-MAKING: ON DEBIASING HUMAN BIASES

One of philosophy's oldest paradoxes is the apparent contradiction between the great triumphs and the dramatic failures of the human mind. The same organism that routinely solves inferential problems too subtle and complex for the mightiest computers often makes errors in the simplest of judgments about everyday events.

Nisbett and Ross (1980)

Our human mind is faulty. We all know it and we all have experienced it. For the sake of efficiency and quick processing, our brain often leads us to make severe misjudgments. You don't think this applies to you? Think again! Have you ever thrown good money after bad, continuing to invest in something because you've already put so much time, effort, or money into it? Even when it was clear that your investment wasn't going to pay off?

Just like feeding the one-armed bandit in a casino more of your money, because maybe next time you will win, and it will be worth all the money you have poured into it? Sound like you? Well, then you have fallen into the trap of the sunk cost fallacy. Or have you ever taken on a big project, such as planning a road trip across the country or renovating a fixer-upper, and felt confident that everything would go smoothly and in just a few months without a hitch? That's an example of optimism bias, a type of cognitive bias that causes us to be overly optimistic about our own future and overlook potential obstacles. It's one of many ways in which our human minds can lead us astray, causing us to believe things that aren't necessarily true or realistic. Clearly, if we base our decisions and judgments on such distorted views, this can have real-world consequences.

For centuries, philosophers have been grappling with the paradox of the human mind. On one hand, we can solve incredibly complex problems, but on the other hand, we make mistakes in our everyday judgments that seem so simple. This is where the field of behavioral economics comes in. This field of study, which combines economics and psychology, was born out of the realization that traditional economic models did not accurately reflect the decision-making patterns of real people in the real world. By studying how we make decisions, behavioral economists have uncovered a number of heuristics, or mental shortcuts, that our brains use to make sense of the world around us. Unfortunately, these shortcuts can sometimes lead to systematic errors in judgment and decision-making, resulting in what are known as cognitive biases. Today we know of more than 180 cognitive biases that influence our thinking and decision-making. They're caused by the way our brains process information, and they can lead us to make irrational or inaccurate decisions.

From the optimism bias to the sunk cost fallacy, cognitive biases can show up in all sorts of day-to-day situations, affecting everything from how we invest our money to how we choose our vacations. For example, the optimism bias is a tendency to be overly optimistic about the likelihood of positive outcomes while downplaying the chances of negative ones. This can cause us to take risks and make choices based on overly positive assumptions. Or the sunk cost fallacy is a tendency to continue investing in something because we've already invested time, money, or effort into it, even if it's not in our best interest to do so.

These biases can be helpful in allowing us to make quick decisions without much mental effort. They help us simplify the incredibly complex world we live in. They also can also motivate us because they can give us a more optimistic outlook on life. However, they can also be dangerous. They can lead us to make choices that are not in our best interest or have negative consequences for us. For example, a person who smokes may feel like their chance of getting cancer is rather low. So the optimism bias causes them to underestimate the risks of their behavior, ultimately leading to risky decisions based on biased expectations. Or a family may decide to drive sixty miles through a bad snowstorm to see a basketball game because they have already made a (sunk) investment of forty dollars per ticket. This is the sunk cost effect in action! It causes us to engage in an action—such as driving through a snowstorm—that we would not engage in if it weren't for our prior investment—such as already having paid for those basketball tickets. As these examples aim to illustrate, more often than not these naturally occurring biases have a degrading effect on our decision quality. Or put differently, these biases often let us make poor choices and bad decisions!

Obviously then it is important to understand these biases and how they work, so we can learn to spot them and make more informed, rational decisions. Indeed, the scientific community agrees so much on the importance of uncovering and understanding these human biases that the "founding fathers of behavioral economics"—Daniel Kahnemann and Richard H. Thaler—both received the Nobel Prize in economics for their groundbreaking research into the irrationality of decision making and the heuristics and biases that influence our thinking. They were among the first to show that our brains rely on shortcuts, or heuristics, to make quick decisions but that these shortcuts often lead to systematic errors, or biases.

Today, we have a good understanding of the many ways in which biases affect our daily decision making. The good news is: awareness is the first step to improvement! If we are aware of our biases, we can also work to overcome them. And that's where the rise of AI comes in. AI can help us reduce these biases by providing us with objective, data-driven insights and alternative perspectives, thereby pointing us to our biases and improving our decision-making.

Picture this: you're in a situation where you're bombarded with information but need to decide quickly. In such a situation, we often fall prey to a confirmation bias, where we only consider information that confirms our prior beliefs. With AI by our side, we can base our decision on information that the AI has (objectively) sorted and analyzed for us. In this way, we can avoid the pitfalls of our intuition and defeat our irrational tendencies to make better and less biased decisions, even when we are pressed for time.

But that's just one example of how AI can drive better decisions. There are more! Remember the sunk cost effect?

Well, a recent study looked at how AI systems can help reduce this fallacy. The study found that when people were asked to decide about whether to continue investing in a project or not, they were less likely to fall into the sunk cost trap when they used an AI system to help them decide. In fact, people who used the system to support them were more likely to make rational decisions about whether or not to continue investing in the project than those who decided all by themselves. Why? The answer is simple: the more work we delegate to AI, the less work we have invested ourselves – and the less we cling to projects. Usually, it's difficult for us to let go when we've invested time, money, or effort into something. But when we collaborate with AI, it simply does not feel like we have made such a big investment. After all, we've delegated part of our efforts to the AI system. Because it doesn't feel like a substantial behavioral investment to us, there are no real (sunk) costs, and as a result, we don't (irrationally) factor them into our decision-making. In short, the less investment we feel we have made, the less we fall victim to the sunk cost fallacy. And AI can help us do that!

But it's not just the sunk cost fallacy that AI can help us overcome. Let us illustrate this with a little story of our own. Recently we set out on a hike up a mountain in the Swiss Alps. At the beginning of the hike, we noticed strong winds and briefly considered whether we should turn back. However, we optimistically decided to continue – not least because we also considered ourselves particularly capable hikers. On our way up the mountain, we encountered other hikers who warned us about dangerous weather conditions. But we ignored their advice and continued, ignoring the clear signs that we should turn back.

Sound familiar? This is a prime example of the optimism bias we discussed before. It's when we feel like we just know something is going to work out well for us, even when all the evidence points to the contrary. It is our tendency to overestimate the likelihood of good things happening and to underestimate the likelihood of bad things happening to us. It causes us to be overoptimistic about ourselves, our skills, and our future. Why else would so many people put money into sweepstakes?

Optimism Bias and Psychological Reactance: A Prime Example of A Cognitive Bias AI Can Help Us With

From research we know that it is really hard to overcome this bias. You may think it is as simple as giving us accurate and objective feedback. Say, the predicted likelihood that we would make it up that mountain. Or telling a smoker about the probability of developing cancer. But here's the thing: there is another bias! Our brains are wired to quickly accept evidence that confirms what we already believe and to assess counterevidence with a highly critical eye. So much so that sometimes we even experience a "boomerang effect" when we hear something we don't like: instead of changing our opinion, we find ourselves becoming even more committed to our original point of view! We come up with new counterarguments to defend our original opinion, making us even more entrenched in our beliefs.

So finding ways to make us learn from feedback in an unbiased manner, to reduce our optimism bias, has been a challenge. But recently a new factor has emerged that may help us solve this challenge: AI advisers! More often than not, people today receive advice from AI rather than human advisers. For example, if we need help buying a house, we can use REX Real Estate or Roof.ai. If we need help with money, we can use Wealthfront, Betterment, or InteractiveAdvisors. AI can even help us find social services such as disability benefits, food assistance, or health insurance. The appeal of these systems is straightforward: As AI bases recommendations on large volumes of data, rather than human intuition, it can provide unbiased advice and help improve our decisions on investing, hiring, lending, or even criminal justice.

But unbiased recommendations are just one crucial ingredient for better decisions. Of course, we must also take the advice! So can AI help us reduce the biased intake of information and thus ultimately the optimism bias?

As there is little to no evidence today that could answer this question, we conducted our own research. Typical of experimental research, our participants were randomly assigned to one of four groups: half received information that disconfirmed their prior beliefs, the other half received information that confirmed their prior beliefs. Half received information from AI, the other half from a human adviser. In reality, and to ensure that our results were not otherwise biased, both groups were given the same advice. But the participants didn't know.

Our results showed something extremely interesting: if participants thought they were talking to a human, their advice-taking was subconsciously biased. Whenever they heard something they liked, they took it to heart and truly believed it. But if they heard something they weren't so fond of, they didn't give it a second thought and ignored the advice. However, when people interacted with AI, they were more unbiased in their reactions to the information and accepted the advice whether they liked it or not. This shows that participants who received advice from the AI were more likely to accept the information – regardless of whether it reinforced or invalidated their beliefs. Ultimately, it was thus also possible to counteract "over-optimism."

That's great news, of course. But—as usual with researchers—we also wanted to understand the "magic sauce." Why are we more accepting of advice from AI? The magic word is "agency." Recall that agency basically refers to people's perception of someone's ability to choose their own paths and take responsibility for the results of their decisions. Do robots have their own motives? Not in our experiment! We purposely tested an AI system without a name or any other human-like features so that participants would not assign much agency to the system. No intentions or feelings, just facts. The opposing advice from the cold and unfeeling machine did not trigger the same emotional response as when the advice was given by a human. In that way we could reduce the optimism bias among participants, something that many researchers have tried to achieve over the past decades.

In Chapter 2, we explained how the perceived agency of an AI system can be varied through design. By giving an AI system names and other human-like features, companies can ensure that we perceive the AI system as more human-like.

Naturally, we wondered how the results of our study would change if we anthropomorphized our AI system. In another experiment, we gave our purely functional AI system a name, a friendly face, and a human-like manner of communication. The participants, of course, still knew they were interacting with a machine and that no human was involved. We wanted to see if simply adding social features would be enough to change the participants' behavior.

Our results confirmed our theory: when the participants interacted with the humanized AI system, they exhibited similar biases as they did with our human advisor previously. In short, negative advice was ignored, and only positive advice was taken into account! Isn't it amazing how a few small changes can completely alter our subconscious behavior?

We put our research to the test by conducting eight additional experiments to ensure our findings were accurate. We examined the effect in other domains, such as real estate, and with a variety of people, even four hundred US executives. Our data from more than ten thousand participants showed that AI systems can indeed help us reduce the optimism bias!

Now let's look at how AI can help us overcome our biases in practical situations, such as in the hiking story we discussed earlier. In this scenario, the optimism bias caused us to overestimate our ability to reach the summit and commit to the hike. When other hikers told us to turn around, we experienced an emotional response and the boomerang effect kicked in, causing us to discredit their message and become even more committed to our original belief. But what if we had asked for advice from a source with a low social agency, such as The Weather Company's Watson? This AI system, developed by IBM, uses machine learning to analyze data from a variety of sources, including weather models, satellites, and ground-based sensors, to generate real-time weather forecasts. Most likely if Watson had alerted us to dangerous weather conditions in our location, it would not have triggered the same emotional response and boomerang effect that the other hikers' advice did. Instead, most likely we would have turned around and it would have prevented us from engaging in such irrational risk-taking. So in short, AI can be a powerful source to debias our decisions!

SUPERCHARGED EFFICIENCY: ON DELEGATING TO AI

Do you ever feel overwhelmed by all the tasks and obligations that come with modern life? From long hours at the office to managing finances and insurance, to taking care of household chores and remembering to get the perfect birthday gift for each and every friend, have you ever felt like it is too much to handle on your own? If so, you are not alone. Many people struggle to juggle all the tasks and obligations of modern life. But what if there was a way to free some time and energy by delegating some of those tasks?

If you think about it, it is possible! One solution might be to delegate tasks to professionals who have the time and skills to handle them more effectively. For example, you might consider hiring a financial planner to manage your finances or a real estate agent to sell your home. By giving up control over these tasks, you'll have more time to sit back, relax, and enjoy the fruits of your labor. In addition, you'll have the added bonus of knowing that everything is being taken care of by someone who knows exactly what they're doing. Sounds pretty straightforward, right?

It may seem surprising, but many people struggle with this decision to delegate, and it's often influenced by our desire to maintain control, as well as by our fear of losing it. So how do we decide whether to retain control or delegate a task? Perhaps it helps to think of the decision as a simple mental calculation. First, we consider the tangible benefits of retaining control. For example, how likely do we think we will succeed and how important is a successful outcome to us? Next, we consider the benefits of delegating the task. So this time we look at the other person's likelihood of success and the value of a successful outcome. But there's one more factor to consider: the "control premium." This represents the value we're willing to forgo to remain in control of a decision, considering the uncertainty and potential suffering that come with handing over control to someone else.

Handing over control to another person is risky. After all, who knows what the other person might be doing behind our backs! The control premium reflects our uncertainty about the other person's knowledge, biases, intentions, and self-interests, as well as the potential suffering we'll experience if things go wrong. The higher the stakes that are involved in the decision, the greater the suffering we're likely to experience if the other person doesn't act in our best interests, and the less willing we are to give up control. In other words: the control premium is based on the uncertainty of losing control and is multiplied by the potential suffering of the worst outcome.

Ultimately, we delegate a task when the value of retaining control is less than the value of delegating minus the control premium. However, in an efficient world, we would delegate when the value of retaining control is simply less than the value of delegating. The control premium represents an efficiency loss that occurs because we're naturally hesitant to give up control. So in essence we deliberately "pay" to maintain control and keep the decision right. This reluctance to delegate decisions can have far-reaching consequences, leading to suboptimal outcomes for individuals, businesses, and society as a whole.

We may be hesitant to delegate tasks to other people, but what if we could delegate to AI? In a previous section, we looked at the benefits of AI advisory systems. Advisory systems, such as decision-support systems, interactive decision aids, and algorithmic advisers, provide guidance and advice to humans, but the final decision is still made by a person.

However, with the advancement of AI, we now have the option to delegate tasks to autonomous AI. These "performative systems" can make their own decisions without any human input. They are able to operate independently and are becoming an increasingly important part of our lives, from self-driving cars to personal assistants that automate mundane tasks. With the rise of performative AI, you can delegate all sorts of tasks—from booking appointments to writing emails—to your personal AI assistant.

Just consider the example of Google assistant. When it was introduced to the public, Google highlighted how the assistant can call your hairdresser, at your request, and naturally converse with your hairdresser to make an appointment for you that matches both yours and the hairdresser's calendars.

Sounds good. But would you delegate tasks to performative AI? How does AI change our perception of control and, as a result, our willingness to delegate decisions and tasks? As the topic of autonomous AI has only recently started to gain momentum, evidence-based answers to these questions are still scarce. That's why we decided to investigate how AI changes our delegation behavior. To do this, we conducted a few experiments in which participants could delegate decisions on small investments to either other people or AI systems.

Our results were astonishing. When participants had the option to delegate to AI, the detrimental control premium was lower. In other words, with AI, our participants subconsciously made more efficient delegation decisions and delegated more tasks than those who could delegate to a human. The riskier the decision, the larger the difference in our participants' willingness to delegate to AI and to humans. This means that, especially for risky decisions—when it really matters to us—AI can help us let go of control and hand it over to expert systems.

But why do delegation decisions improve when we interact with AI? The results of our experiments suggest that the answer lies in the difference between objectively being in control and subjectively feeling in control. When we delegate to AI, we feel like we are still in control over the task, even though objectively we are not. Imagine you're in the kitchen, ready to whip up your favorite dish for your upcoming birthday party. You've got all the ingredients laid out in front of you, and you're just about to get started when you have a brilliant idea: why not delegate the task to someone else, so you can focus on more important tasks to set the scene for the party? So you hand the recipe over to your friend and ask them to give it a go. While your friend gets started, you can't help but feel a little anxious. You're not sure if they'll follow the recipe exactly—that is, use the right quantities, follow the steps in the correct order, and use the correct temperature. Maybe you even think that your friend will not put their full heart into it—after all, you just learned that there is this big thing at work coming up. In short, you are uncertain if the end result will be as delicious as you know it could be. You feel like you've lost control of the situation. Let's imagine the same situation again, but this time you have decided to delegate the task to your trusted Thermomix instead. You input the recipe and let the machine do its thing. As it whirs and whizzes away, you feel a sense of control knowing that it will follow the instructions to the letter. After all, you still feel in control over the task.

Upon closer look, we see that we were not objectively in control in any of these situations. However, as our research shows, our perception of control can be influenced by who or what we delegate a task to. It's all about our subjective feeling of control, not about actually being in control. Do you see the difference? When it comes to AI, it seems that we feel more in control, even though we're not actually in control of the process. This is because AI systems are perceived to have less intentional capacity, or less agency, than other people. As a result, delegating tasks to AI doesn't undermine our own sense of autonomy the way that delegating tasks to other people can.

A recent study on computer games shows results that point in a similar direction. While participants were playing the game, they received the help of two different digital assistants: for half of the participants, the digital helper was anthropomorphized; for the other half it was pure functional facts. While the game designers assumed that the humanized digital helper must be more liked and accepted, the reverse was true. Indeed, players were more likely to get the help of a very functional helper assisting them during the game. Why is this so? Again, when the assistant was not humanized it left the players' sense of autonomy intact. Put differently, they still felt in control of the game, which, in this case, ultimately led to greater enjoyment of the game—and its adviser!

But here's the catch: AI systems might not have their own intentions, but they don't operate in a vacuum either. Most of the time, AI systems are set up by companies or other organizations that have their own goals and intentions with these systems. So even though the AI itself might not be driven by any particular desire or ambition, it's still acting in service of something bigger. Take the Thermomix, for example. It's just a machine. It doesn't have any desires or goals of its own. But the people who designed and built it might have had all sorts of motivations and intentions. Maybe they wanted to create the most energy-efficient kitchen appliance on the market, sacrificing taste. Or maybe they wanted to make sure their own recipes always came out on top (even if it meant tweaking the machine's programming a little). You see what we are getting at? Technically, delegating a decision to AI should entail uncertainty about the intentions and goal alignments as well.

So we ran another study, but this time we made it crystal clear to our participants that both the human and the AI were acting on behalf of a firm. Did this make a difference in delegation choices? Actually, no! Even when we spelled it out for our participants, they were still more willing to delegate the decision to the AI rather than the human. Our research demonstrates that the belief that only humans, not machines, can act with intention leads to uncertainty about the goals of the agent, which causes people to require a greater expected benefit before entrusting tasks to human agents rather than AI agents. This is because we do not perceive losing as much control over decisions when we delegate them to AI as compared to humans, even if both act on behalf of someone else.

Overall, delegation to performative AI can be extremely empowering. It is a great chance for us to focus our time and energy on the most important aspects of our lives. Think about it: Google assistant can call your hairdresser and book an appointment for you, using a human-like voice. Or ChatGPT can help you write emails faster and with less stress. The Nest Thermostat can even learn your temperature preferences and adjust itself accordingly! With these tools you can spend your time and energy on things that matter most to you. When you delegate such tasks to AI, you're not only saving time but also gaining a sense of empowerment. By not having to do everything yourself, you can focus on activities that you enjoy or that you're good at. This can help you feel more satisfied with your life and increase your self-esteem. However, there is a fine line between delegation and overreliance on AI. Too much delegation can lead to a decrease in our ability to perform tasks ourselves, which can lead to a negative impact on our self-efficacy and sense of control. That's why it's important for us to find the right balance and ensure that we don't become too reliant on AI to the point where it replaces our own capabilities.

CREATIVITY UNLEASHED: THE ART OF CREATING ART WITH AI

We are living in a world where technology can create images so realistic, they are indistinguishable from reality. A world where anything you can dream up can be brought to life with just a few clicks of a button. This is the world of generative AI, and it's a world that is rapidly changing the way we think about creativity and the value of human talent. It is quickly becoming comparable to or, argued by some, better than the average human creation, along with also being faster and cheaper. Generative AI is changing the creative landscape in remarkable ways, revolutionizing the way artists, writers, and musicians work. By leveraging vast amounts of data, generative AI algorithms can produce new and original works that are both innovative and captivating.

In the art world, generative AI is being used to create mesmerizing visuals, with AI-generated paintings and sculptures becoming increasingly popular. Using machine learning techniques, AI models can analyze existing artworks and create unique pieces that mimic the style of famous artists, or even develop entirely new styles. Similarly, in the world of music, generative AI is transforming the way we create and experience sound. With AI-generated compositions, musicians can explore new genres and styles, combining elements from various musical traditions to produce innovative and captivating tracks. Even in the realm of writing, generative AI is making waves. With language models that can generate coherent and nuanced text, writers can now automate parts of the creative process, producing works that are not only engaging but also unique.

While some fear that generative AI may replace human creativity, many artists and creatives see it as a powerful tool that can be used to augment and enhance their own work. By collaborating with AI models, artists can push the boundaries of their craft, opening up new possibilities and creating works that were previously unimaginable.

Indeed, the results of a recent study have shown that AI can truly enhance human creativity. In the study, fifty design students were given an AI partner to work with during a design task, and the results were pretty amazing. The AI tool helped the students generate more ideas and overcome "design fixation"—the tendency to get stuck on the first few ideas that come to mind. Essentially, the tool encouraged a more open-minded approach to design, allowing for both "combinational creativity" (adding more structure to initial designs) and "transformational creativity" (inspiring new features from a completely different design space).

But it's not just a one-way street. In fact, it turns out that humans can also help enhance AI creativity. Recent studies have shown that when humans collaborate with AI on creative tasks, they can achieve better results than when AI works alone. Why? Well, an art piece created by AI may be indistinguishable from that of a human artist. But in the end, people's attitudes and biases toward art created by machines can significantly influence how they evaluate it. For example, in one study, researchers conducted an online survey with 446 participants to investigate how people perceive creative content created by AI. They found that people generally had a negative perception of music created by AI and were unlikely to purchase it. However, when participants were told that the creation involved a human music professional, their biases disappeared. Another group of researchers conducted a study comparing the reactions of people toward creative content created solely by AI versus content created through human-AI collaboration. The results were fascinating. Computer programs were able to write poems that were just as good as those written by humans, and people even enjoyed reading them. However, when a human was involved in the creative process of the poems, people were more likely to think the poems were written by humans and improved the perceived quality of the poems. In other words, people's perceptions of AI creativity are heavily influenced by whether or not a human is involved in the creative process.

So how does creativity unleashed with generative AI work?

To begin, a human must provide a prompt for the generative AI model to create content. A prompt is a sentence with four hundred characters or fewer that describes what you want. The quality of the prompt can greatly impact the quality of the output. So we humans need to get creative here, and the process of creating high-quality output from generative AI is becoming a highly valued skill. In fact, a new profession is emerging that could shape the future of creativity: the "prompt engineer" or the "prompt artist." These digital wizards are the ones responsible for crafting the prompts that trigger AI models to create everything from images to videos. But what does it take to be a prompt engineer? Well, it's a bit like being a composer, but instead of writing music, you're creating the notes that AI follows. And with an eighty-two-page book of DALL-E 2 image prompts already in existence, and even a prompt marketplace where you can buy prompts made by others, it's clear that the field is growing fast. For example, PromptBase is a unique marketplace designed for artists to sell prompts that generate simple images such as emoticons, logos, icons, avatars, and even game weapons. These prompts are easy to use and can be easily tweaked and altered to fit your exact needs. And the best part? You can generate multiple versions of the same image using just one prompt.

The prompts on PromptBase sell for just a few dollars, which is a steal considering the amount of work that goes into creating a good prompt. And a good prompt doesn't just include the subject, but also the lighting, point of view, emotion evoked, color palette, degree of abstraction, and even a reference picture to imitate. But even with all of these incredible tools at our disposal, finding the perfect prompt can still be a challenge.

Once the model generates content, a human can carefully evaluate and edit it to create something truly unique and exceptional. Take Jason Allen, for example, who used a generative AI model to win a Colorado "digitally manipulated photography" contest. He spent over eighty hours refining the model's output, trying out more than nine hundred different versions of his art until he found just the right one. But even then, he wasn't done. Allen used other AI tools to further enhance the image quality and sharpness before finally printing it on canvas.

It's a bit like performing a magic spell. You start by whispering the secret incantations that have worked in the past and add them to the prompt. Then you repeat, change the word order, and remember to be specific. Keep repeating until you have a tribe of images that seem to have good bones and potential. Now it's time to be ruthless and select only the best of the best. Next, you'll use your artistic prowess to bring out the best in the most promising images. You can ask the AI to extend the image out in certain directions beyond its current borders, erase any parts that aren't working, and suggest replacements to be done by the AI with more incantations (called inpainting). If the AI isn't understanding your hints, you can try spells used by others. Once the AI has gone as far as it can, you'll migrate the image to Photoshop for some final touches. It's not uncommon for a distinctive image to require fifty steps. It's a testament to the power of collaboration between humans and AI, and a reminder that even the most advanced technology still needs our guidance and expertise.

Let's illustrate this process. Imagine you want to have an illustration of an artist drawing a robot. A basic prompt such as "illustration of artist drawing a robot" in DALL-E 2 will give you the following results:

Not quite a masterpiece? Don't worry, we can fix that! With a little tweaking of our prompt, we can turn a basic image into a true masterpiece. This time let's try "an illustration from behind of a female artist creating a vivid painting on a canvas of a robot on a white background, digital art, fashion illustration inspired by vogue." Ta-da! Check out these stunning results:

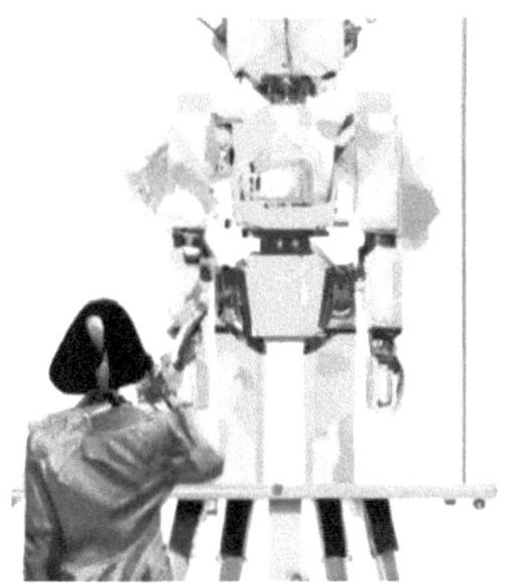 

Knowing the ins and outs of prompting is like upgrading from a finger-painting hobbyist to a Michelangelo of AI—it makes a world of difference! As with any other artistic skill, it takes practice and patience to master the finer points of prompting, as the prompt truly matters.

The best outcomes result from long conversations between humans and machines. However, commanding the AI to perform specific tasks requires a delicate balance of persuasion and patience. Commands such as "shade this area," "enhance this part," and "tone it down" are followed reluctantly. The AIs have to be persuaded. Those who have mastered the algorithms can produce images with visual boldness and coherence that are many times better than the average person's and stand out among the flood of details the AI tends to generate.

In the world of AI-generated art, some artists guard their prompts like top-secret recipes, while others see the process as a thrilling creative journey. Robyn Miller, the mastermind behind the classic game Myst, posts a new AI-generated masterpiece each day and says that there is an art to it that has surprised even him. Meanwhile, artists such as Klingemann believe that all images already exist, and the art is in discovering them rather than sharing the prompts that led to their creation. As you can see, these AI tools will transform creative industries.

As the process described shows, AI generators are not a threat to creative jobs, but partners and transformers. In the past, technology has often supplemented and transformed human labor. For example, the invention of the camera was feared to put portrait painters out of work in the 1800s; the rise of smartphones and amateur photography was feared to reduce professional photography jobs. But instead of putting people out of their jobs, technology has transformed jobs. Just think about it: who would have dreamed of becoming a social media influencer a hundred years ago? In just the same way, who would have thought about becoming a "prompt engineer" just a few years ago? You see, AI is not here to replace human creativity. It will transform it. It is going to change the way we design everything, but not necessarily in a bad way. AI will take over the mundane, repetitive, and ordinary creative tasks, which is a big deal, as it allows us to delegate everyday acts of creativity on demand, in real time, at scale, and at much lower prices.

In the end, the true magic happens when human artists collaborate with AI to bring their visions to life. It's a partnership that requires an understanding of the unique strengths and limitations of both the artist and the technology. With AI's ability to quickly generate a wide range of possibilities, artists are freed to focus on refining and enhancing their creations. It's like having a team of assistants who can handle the mundane tasks while the artist focuses on the truly creative aspects of their work. In short, it is creativity unleashed!

CHAPTER 4

THE BIG BUT: THE HIDDEN RISKS OF TEAMING UP WITH "RATIONAL AI"

We've all heard the promises of AI revolutionizing our lives and making the world a better place, but there's another side to this shiny technological coin. Welcome to the downsides of teaming up with "rational AI." In this chapter we'll explore the various ways AI can actually do more harm than good.

In particular, we'll discuss how AI bias and discrimination can perpetuate existing biases in society and lead to greater inequality. This happens when AI systems are trained on biased data, which teaches them to associate certain demographic characteristics with certain traits or behaviors, even if these characteristics don't have any causal relationship. This can result in self-fulfilling prophecies and create further inequalities.

We will discuss how filter bubbles, which are created when AI algorithms personalize content based on our online behavior, can limit our exposure to new ideas and perspectives. While this personalization might seem convenient, it also means that we're only exposed to a narrow and homogenous view of the world, limiting our understanding and knowledge of different perspectives.

This brings us to the next point: how does AI change the way we think and solve problems? We will critically discuss how AI systems can manipulate our behavior and emotions in subtle ways. This can happen when AI systems use algorithms to optimize content and experiences for engagement and click-through rates, often at the expense of our well-being. This can result in what's been called "mind hacking," where AI systems can change our thoughts, emotions, and even our beliefs without us even realizing it.

And we will look at what happens when we rely too heavily on Google and other search engines to remember things for us. While AI systems make it easier for us to access information quickly, it also can affect our memory. When we're relying on AI to remember things for us, we're less likely to recall information, and this can impact our cognitive abilities and overall brain function.

Last, we will dive into how delegating too much to AI and letting AI take over tasks that once required human effort and skill could make us lazy and lead to a critical process of human "deskilling" and the effects AI has on human cooperation.

From algorithmic bias and discrimination to filter bubbles, AI as a mind hacker and the Google effect on memory, we'll delve into the very real dangers of relying too heavily on our new best buddy: AI. Why do all this? Taking a more critical view can help us be more mindful of the ways AI affects us and ensures that we can use AI appropriately and responsibly.

THE MYTH OF THE RATIONAL, NEUTRAL ALGORITHM

It's no secret that humans aren't always the most unbiased creatures. In fact, we're prone to making decisions based on our own personal biases and prejudices. Researchers have found that judges' decisions can be influenced by their own characteristics, and employers have been known to grant interviews to certain candidates at higher rates just because of their names, which are believed to reflect certain racial groups. And let's not even get started on how humans can misuse information when making decisions. Have you heard about how some employers use credit histories to judge job candidates, even though there's no proven link between credit history and job performance? This can be especially unfair to minority groups. It can be tough to figure out exactly what went into a human's decision-making process too— people might not be totally honest about what factors they considered, or they might not even realize what influenced their thinking. All of this can leave a lot of room for unconscious bias.

But these are all problems of the past! Humans' implicit biases can from now on be eliminated by AI. This is because AI systems have a superior capacity for processing or detecting patterns from large amounts of information. Unlike humans, who tend to simplify decisions through the use of heuristics, algorithms can consider a large number of observations of an equally large number of variables to come up with accurate and data-driven predictions. So all in all, AI agents can provide fairer evaluations, sidestepping human biases, and ultimately reducing—or even eliminating—discrimination . . . or so we thought. But as we've come to learn more about how these algorithms work, it's become clear that the reality is a bit more complex.

Unfortunately, there is a strong argument that algorithms might also preserve—or even amplify—systematic discrimination perpetuated by humans. Many modern algorithms are built to likely replicate any human biases embedded in their training data sets. In short: garbage in—garbage out! So if the data is biased, then the AI system will be biased as well. And that complete, accurate, and unbiased dataset that rationality requires does not exist. The data we use to train our models has been influenced by humans making questionable decisions, or by larger systems of inequality that have played out over time.

For example, an algorithm trained on a data set in which men received better performance evaluations than women will use gender as a factor in making predictions about how future candidates will perform. If the association in the training data set was due to the managers' biases—that is, if there is no gender-performance link in objective reality—an algorithm has no way of detecting this pattern and therefore might blithely replicate this unfair bias. Similarly, if in the past certain ethnicities were denied loans more frequently, then the AI system will "sniff out" this pattern in the data and replicate it. The system may pick up on statistical correlations that are socially unacceptable or illegal. It won't be doing this because it's intrinsically evil (AI systems don't have morals), but rather because it's trying to achieve the highest prediction accuracy based on the data it was given.

Unfortunately, documented cases of algorithmic discrimination have already emerged. For example, the algorithm COMPAS, used across the United States to predict whether specific parolees were likely to reoffend, showed a racially biased pattern of errors: its most common mistake was to miscategorize black defendants as likely to reoffend when ultimately, they did not. Amazon also stopped development of a HR hiring algorithm after noticing that it penalized résumés that mentioned the word "women." Even if organizations attempt to withhold demographic information from their algorithms, this information is often contained in proxy variables (such as names and zip codes).

And the list does not end there. Facial recognition systems used in law enforcement, which are supposed to keep us safe, struggle when it comes to recognizing faces of women and Black individuals. Natural language processing algorithms have been found to encode language in a gendered way. And if that wasn't enough, consider this: if you search for a name that sounds distinctly Black, you are more likely to be served ads for arrest records. And if you are a woman, you are less likely to see ads for high- paying jobs. Even if ad postings are crafted to be gender neutral, algorithms prioritize men for job postings in science, technology, engineering, and math-related (STEM) fields.

Clearly, such bias in AI systems can have severe consequences for both the individuals who are discriminated against and for society as a whole. It undermines people's ability to fully participate in the economy and society. Just consider this: women who never see the job posting about a well-paid job in science or engineering will never apply, even if they might be just as right for the job as a man who gets to see the ad. So even though encouraging women to enter the STEM field might be a priority in a society, the use of AI systems that are trained on biased data, or that optimize for the "wrong" outcome, can perpetuate and even amplify discrimination at scale.

But how does AI even reinforce discrimination?

Just imagine you're a real estate agent looking to make a killing in the property market. You decide to use the latest and greatest AI technology to predict which neighborhoods will experience a surge in property values over the next year. You feed the machine learning model mountains of data, including information about the demographics of each neighborhood, the quality of local schools, and other factors that may affect property values. But little do you know, the data you fed the model is biased. It reflects the prejudices and biases of the people who collected it. So the model starts associating certain demographic characteristics with lower property values, even if these characteristics don't have any causal relationship with property values.

Armed and ready with the predictions of the AI model—and utterly unsuspecting of what's going on in the background—you're ready to make some serious cash. You start buying properties in neighborhoods that are predicted to have higher property values, and you avoid those that are predicted to have lower property values. But what you don't realize is that your decisions, based on the predictions of the AI model, could be causing a cycle of disinvestment in certain neighborhoods. Real estate investors and agents, following your lead, start avoiding neighborhoods that are predicted to have lower property values. This disinvestment leads to a decline in the quality of schools and other amenities in these neighborhoods, which further decreases property values and perpetuates the cycle of bias. The AI model's predictions become a self-fulfilling prophecy, and the neighborhoods that were already struggling continue to struggle.

Or imagine you're a police officer trying to keep the streets safe. To help you out, the department gives you an AI system that predicts criminal behavior. You're thinking, "Sweet, this will make my job a whole lot easier!" But little do you know, the system is trained on data from a city where one of your colleagues holds biases against a certain ethnic group. As a result, this officer disproportionately arrests individuals from this group. The AI system, being a machine, doesn't know any better and starts associating individuals from this group with criminal behavior, even if they haven't actually done anything wrong. Now all officers in the city start using this system, which tells them that individuals from this particular group are more likely to commit crimes. Suddenly you and your colleagues are more likely to stop, frisk, and arrest individuals from this group, simply because the AI system said so. This can lead to a self-fulfilling prophecy, where these individuals are more likely to be arrested, convicted, and imprisoned simply because of the bias in the AI system. Even officers who don't hold biases against this group may unknowingly act in a biased manner because the system is telling them to do so.

In the end, this can perpetuate discrimination and inequality as the system continues to learn from more and more biased data. It can also enhance biases among officers, as the biased officer may feel more justified in their beliefs about the group and even unbiased officers may start to believe there may be a correlation between ethnicity and criminal behavior, which could lead to racism. So the AI system that was supposed to make the officer's job easier ended up making it more complicated, and even more dangerous for certain communities.

These examples illustrate how AI systems can perpetuate and even amplify human biases, leading to greater discrimination and inequality. It's important to remember that AI systems are not neutral, and they can only be as unbiased as the data they are trained on. However, despite the evidence that algorithms can and do discriminate, this reality has not made it into our heads. Instead, we often tend to prefer algorithmic judgment over human judgment, especially if we expect to be discriminated against. And if we receive the identical advice from an AI instead of a human, we perceive it as less discriminating—even if it is!

So why do we sometimes hold on to the belief that algorithms and AI are less discriminatory than humans? As we now know, this belief does not emerge from objective truth but rather from psychological factors such as our intuitions, theories, and stereotypes about machines (remember our discussions in chapter 2!). These factors can lead people to conclude that algorithms are relatively unlikely to discriminate.

One reason for this false belief is that we perceive algorithms as exceptionally accurate, or able to detect patterns to determine "real" values of what they are trying to predict. We tend to think of AI systems as relatively agentic agents capable of calculation. We might also correctly recognize that algorithms are able to parse patterns that would escape a mere person; indeed, this capability is one of the driving forces behind the automation of decision-making. Human evaluators, on the other hand, tend to appear more prone to error, perhaps because we know others' judgments sometimes rely on shortcuts and extraneous factors, potentially including biased stereotypes.

So where do these assumptions about machines leave us? Well, if AI agents appear more accurate and less emotional evaluators than humans, we may easily assume that their recommendations are less discriminating and fairer compared to humans making those exact same recommendations. And this is precisely what psychologists found. Across seven separate studies, the researchers tested people's reaction to hiring advice made either by a human hiring manager or by an algorithm driven by AI. The advice was always identical. And discriminating. So, out of the two job referrals the participants saw, the advice would always favor the Caucasian male over a female or non-Caucasian applicant. Despite clearly being discriminating in their advice, people perceived the algorithm's recommendation as less discriminatory than the human hiring manager's.

Why? In essence, participants assumed that algorithms are more accurate and less emotional evaluators and thus less likely to make discriminatory decisions. And this preference for AI evaluators does not only apply when we think others are being judged. In fact, the research team was also able to show that people prefer an AI assessment especially when they expect to be discriminated against themselves. This, too, is rooted in the belief that the algorithm will be more impartial and unbiased.

Clearly these beliefs can be dangerous. They might lead us to blindly seek algorithmic evaluation in situations where such technologies maintain or even amplify discrimination while simultaneously obscuring it. So people, groups, organizations, and social systems (e.g., governments and courtrooms) need only emphasize their use of technology to make decisions look just and fair, even though they may be discriminatory. And as our prior discussion shows, this might just work. We feel better and may be less likely to react to being discriminated against if we believe that a (neutral) AI is making decisions or is heavily involved in the evaluation process.

In our daily lives, algorithms are increasingly being used to help us make decisions. However, we should keep in mind that these technologies are not always accurate and unbiased. In fact, many real-world applications have shown that AI systems can be just as biased as humans. Therefore, it's important for us to be aware that we shouldn't blindly rely on algorithmic recommendations, especially when it comes to decisions about people. These decision-making processes can both mask (by keeping discriminatory associations opaque) and scale (a single algorithm such as COMPAS can serve many jurisdictions) discrimination.

The myth of the neutral and unbiased algorithm is just that—a myth. Therefore, it is crucial to be aware of the potential biases in algorithms and take them into consideration when using AI-generated results. So before you make a decision based on algorithms the next time, think twice and be aware that your assumptions about the accuracy and impartiality of this advice may not always be correct.

PERSONALIZED IS GOOD? ON GETTING TRAPPED IN A BUBBLE OF YOUR OWN

We've all been there: scrolling through our social media feeds or browsing our favorite news sites, searching for interesting articles. Whether we're waiting in line at the grocery store, procrastinating at work, or trying to fall asleep, we can't resist the allure of the endless scroll.

But have you ever stopped to think about the forces that are shaping the information you see online? Have you ever noticed that the more you use the internet, the more it seems to know exactly what you want? That's because personalized filters driven by AI are at work, tailoring your online experience to your individual interests and habits, and designed to be as addictive as possible to get you to keep clicking. This can result in a "filter bubble," a unique universe of information that is tailored specifically to your interests and preferences. You're bombarded with articles and posts that already align with your beliefs and confirm your opinions.

At first this may seem like a dream come true. No more sifting through articles that don't interest you or coming across perspectives that challenge your beliefs. But as it turns out, this personalized paradise can lead to a sort of radicalization. By only exposing us to information that aligns with our existing beliefs, these filter bubbles can prevent us from encountering new ideas and perspectives. We may find ourselves becoming more entrenched in our views and less open to differing opinions. And before we know it, we're stuck in our own little echo chamber, isolated from the diverse and complex world around us.

You may think that you've heard about this phenomenon long before the rise of algorithms, as humans have always tended to seek information and opinions that align with their own beliefs. But this time it's different. We're experiencing a revolutionary change in the way we consume media, with the rise of algorithmic personalization. In traditional media selection, we chose our preferred sources ourselves. For example, a conservative person might read Fox News, while a liberal one might read The Nation. But algorithms are now able to tailor the information and news we see, to an extent never seen before. This means we're no longer just choosing the media that aligns with our beliefs, the media is being chosen for us.

Imagine it like this: you walk into a vast library and find only books tailored to your interests and reading habits. That sounds great, but what if you don't even know that you're being presented with a limited selection?

In fact, there are two types of personalization: explicit and implicit. With explicit personalization, we actively tell the algorithm what we like—for example, by filtering romantic comedies on a streaming service. The service then gives us a list of recommendations based on the specific criteria we provided. In contrast, implicit personalization involves the algorithm tracking our activities and deducing our preferences without us realizing. So if we watch a 90s romantic comedy, the service might recommend similar movies, assuming we enjoy that type of film. In both cases, the selection of movies is personalized. However, with explicit personalization, we consciously choose to encounter like-minded opinions and risk receiving biased and one-dimensional information. In contrast, implicit personalization functions without our choice, input, knowledge, and consent. We don't even know we're receiving biased information, and thus may become trapped in a filter bubble.

It's important to understand these two types of personalization because it's not just about convenience or even personalization, but it also has a big impact on how we understand the world around us. The more we rely on these algorithms to curate our information, the more we risk being trapped in a "filter bubble" where we are only exposed to information that confirms our existing beliefs and perspectives and being insulated from any alternative viewpoint. It's a fine line between simplifying our lives and limiting our understanding of the world. The critical issue of personalization in the era of big data is that the crucial difference between individual selection and automatic functioning, which is beyond the influence of human will, is blurred.

In the digital world, companies are constantly competing for our attention, time, and engagement. They make money by monetizing our attention. The more time we spend online on their websites and platforms, the more money they make from advertising placements and offers. To captivate us and distract us from other things, they deliver only what they believe will appeal to us. Algorithms, therefore, continually collect data about us to better know what we want, perhaps even more than we do ourselves. They provide us with implicitly personalized content that we may like but not necessarily what we need to see. We don't know the criteria by which these algorithms judge us and what we may be missing out on. As a result, we find ourselves in an automatically generated filter bubble without realizing it. We should be aware that algorithms show only what they think we want to see, not necessarily what is important.

Every technological advancement comes with a multitude of pros and cons, some of which may not become apparent until later. Algorithmic personalization can make it easier to find relevant information, but it can also have harmful effects and raise moral and societal concerns.

When we are trapped in these bubbles, we are cut off from opposing viewpoints and perspectives, giving us the false impression that our own narrow self-interest is the only thing that exists. This can lead to increased polarization and a lack of ability to compromise or understand alternative perspectives. As a result of filter bubbles, we may develop the belief that our opinion is the only correct one, since we are not exposed to any differing viewpoints or counterarguments. We assume that everyone else is seeing the same information we are, and therefore that our perspective must be the right one. As individuals on both sides of an issue become more entrenched in their own positions, effective conversations and solution-finding become increasingly difficult.

This issue has implications for our personal relationships as well as for society and democracy. In our personal relationships and national arguments, polarization can make it hard to have respectful and productive conversations with those holding different views. It's because it seems like they are living in a "different world." However, we are all living in our own little bubble world where all we see is what we want to see and all we hear is what we want to hear. This creates an even deeper divide between people with opposing views and increases the difficulty of reaching common ground. This growing divide is evident in political parties, which are increasingly moving further apart rather than coming together. This is not just an abstract concept, it's a real-world issue that affects our everyday interactions. If left unaddressed, it can escalate to hostility and even violence. That's not only detrimental to our personal growth and relationships; it also messes with democracy.

For democracy to function properly, it's essential that all citizens have access to accurate and diverse information and can engage in meaningful conversations about the issues at hand. However, filter bubbles can prevent this from happening by blocking access to crucial information and new perspectives. They prioritize content that is deemed personally relevant to us—and, even more importantly, that can achieve a high number of clicks and other forms of user engagement. What they do not prioritize is content that might be relevant, even important for social cohesion and that are verified facts. As you can imagine, all this together makes it harder for individuals to make informed decisions about the issues they are voting on.

The US election in 2016 and the Brexit vote have sparked intense discussions on the impact of filter bubbles on the results. The outcomes of these events came as a surprise to many, with even those in the political and journalistic communities expecting a different outcome. While the influence of filter bubbles in shaping these historical events is a subject that is still being studied and debated, research has found general evidence proving a polarizing effect of filter bubbles on voting behavior.

Are you ready for the alarming truth? Studies show that the search results you see online can influence your voting decision. In fact, experiments have demonstrated that altering search results can increase the voting preferences of undecided voters by a staggering 20 percent or more. But it's not just the general population that's affected; certain demographic groups experience even greater shifts in their opinions. The worst part is that these manipulations are so subtle that most people aren't even aware of them. Scientists have dubbed this phenomenon the "search engine manipulation effect," and it can influence attitudes and beliefs beyond just politics. With election outcomes often determined by slim margins, the ability of a single search engine company to influence the results of countless elections is a chilling thought, particularly in countries where one company dominates internet search. We live in a world where the power to sway elections lies not in the hands of political campaigns but in the hands of the company controlling your internet search.

Taken to the extreme, evidence shows that filter bubbles can lead to radicalization. This is due to the unconscious reinforcement of certain patterns of behavior that happens without user knowledge or consent. To highlight the moral and societal implications of algorithmic personalization, consider the case of Charleston church shooter Dylan Roof. He was a more passive internet user, and his radicalization began when he searched for "black on White crime" on Google, getting trapped in a filter bubble of racist content. As he himself stated, he "has never been the same" since that experience. This illustrates how algorithmic personalization can influence individual decision-making and how that can be a source of public concern.

As you can see, filter bubbles can have detrimental consequences on us and on society. Breaking free from them is an important task that requires the cooperation of various stakeholders. The creators of social media platforms and other sources of information hold a significant responsibility in this regard. If algorithms are going to be the gatekeepers of the information we consume, it's crucial that they not only select content based on relevance (and the potential to be monetized), but also present us with ideas that might be uncomfortable, thought-provoking, significant, or different perspectives. They have a duty to create unbiased websites and to keep their algorithms in check so that we don't end up surrounded by "information junk food" instead of a balanced diet of news and perspectives. As the famous internet activist Pariser puts it, "the best editing gives us a bit of both . . . information vegetables and information dessert."

But it's not just up to them; schools and other educational institutions also play a crucial role in raising awareness about the dangers of filter bubbles and demonstrating how to avoid or break free from them. By increasing awareness of the existence and consequences of filter bubbles, they can equip people with the necessary tools to recognize and counter them. This includes teaching critical thinking, research skills, and media literacy so that people can evaluate the information they are presented with, understand the potential biases of different sources, and seek out a diversity of perspectives.

Finally, everyone also has a responsibility to take ownership of their online experience and actively work to break free from their own filter bubbles. Recognizing that you're in a filter bubble is the first step in escaping it. It's like being in your own movie, like Truman, and not even noticing it, but once you become aware of it, you can start planning a way out.

One way to snap out of the filter bubble is to actively seek out diverse perspectives and information. You can do this by deliberately exposing yourself to news, opinions, and ideas from sources that you would not normally consume. You can follow social media accounts, news outlets, or online communities that differ from your usual preferences; attend events or lectures by people with diverse perspectives; or even travel to new places and meet new people.

Another way to break out of the filter bubble is using the incognito browsing mode, which allows you to surf the internet without leaving any trace of your browsing history on your device. Additionally, avoiding logging into your accounts on different websites or deleting your search history can also help to break out of the filter bubble. By adjusting the settings on your social media accounts and web browsers, for example, you can further limit the influence of algorithms and ensure that you're being exposed to a wider range of information.

Finally, deleting or blocking browser cookies is another way to escape the bubble. Websites typically use cookies, which are small text files, to keep track of our browsing history and tailor the content they show us. By manually deleting these cookies or using browser extensions to remove them, you can break free of the filter bubble. However, cookies can be useful, so it's recommended to use discretion when deleting them.

In the end, we must be aware that these personalized filters can cut us off from new ideas and perspectives. We should actively seek out diverse viewpoints and critically question our information diet. We should learn to diversify our information sources to promote our mental flexibility and openness. It's crucial for people to have access to diverse, unbiased, and accurate information. Breaking through filter bubbles, therefore, is a collective task that requires collaboration from social media platforms, educational institutions, and individuals alike. Only through joint efforts can we counteract the negative effects of filter bubbles caused by AI-driven personalization and promote an open and informed society.

THE AI MIND HACKER: HOW ARTIFICIAL INTELLIGENCE IS PLAYING YOU LIKE A PRO

We exploited Facebook to harvest millions of people's profiles and built models to exploit what we knew about them and target their inner demons. That was the basis the entire company was built on.

Christopher Wylie,
one of Cambridge Analytica's cofounders-
turned-whistleblower (2018)

Imagine a world where every click, every search, and every like you make online is being recorded, analyzed, and used to create a digital version of you. That's right—your digital footprint! But it gets even more interesting. Imagine a technology that creates a psychological profile of you so accurately that it is able to control your every move, guiding you toward certain actions without you even realizing it.

Sounds like something straight out of a science fiction novel, right? But this is not just a figment of our imagination. AI is becoming increasingly better at influencing our decisions—and as we are often completely unaware that this is happening! And that's where things start to get a little dicey. As AI becomes so sophisticated and sneaky in its influence, the line between personalization and manipulation starts to blur. The application of AI in targeted advertising and political campaigns, such as the infamous Cambridge Analytica case, is a prime example of how AI can shape our preferences and goals and nudge our behaviors in a certain direction.

Just think about it: have you ever felt like your computer or smartphone is controlling your every move? A study in 2020 may just confirm your suspicions. This study presented three experiments that showcase just how powerful AI can be in influencing our behavior.

In the first experiment, participants had to go through a series of trials in which they had to choose between two squares on a screen to earn virtual money. After each choice, they were given feedback in the form of either a happy face (indicating they had earned a reward) or a sad face (meaning they had not earned a reward). The catch is that an AI system assigned the rewards (or not) to the two fields before each choice. By learning the participants' choice patterns, the AI arranged these rewards so participants would choose the option that was predefined as the "target" option. Despite the AI being tasked with assigning exactly twenty-five rewards to each square, it managed to get people to choose the target option 70 percent of the time. It's as if the AI could read their minds!

In the second experiment, participants were asked to press a button when they saw a particular symbol (like an orange triangle) and not press it when they saw another (like a blue circle). The AI system arranged the sequence of symbols in a way that led to almost 25 percent more errors by the participants. It was like the AI was playing a game of cat and mouse with the participants' minds, and it was winning.

In the third experiment, participants acted as investors and provided funds to an AI system acting as a trustee. The trustee would then return a portion of the investment, and the participant would decide how much to invest in the next round. The study included two different modes of play. In one mode, the AI aimed to maximize its own profit, while in the other, it aimed for a fair distribution of money between itself and the participant. The AI system was successful in both modes of play. It was as if the AI was manipulating the participants into making the choices it wanted them to make for it to achieve its goal.

Clearly, these experimental setups are still quite artificial. After all, we don't sit at our computers pressing buttons when we see a certain symbol pop up. Nevertheless, these studies show how well AI can detect and exploit human weaknesses in decision-making to persuasively guide people toward certain decisions or actions. Similar to a skilled salesperson or persuasive trickster getting you to take an action, AI can also prompt you to click, purchase, or share content. This is not only because AI possesses a significant amount of knowledge about you, but also because it has insight into the techniques that are likely to sway your decision in a particular direction at just the right moment.

All of this may seem like something out of a dystopian novel, but AI-driven influence is real and happening now. For example, through analyzing data, AI discovered that negative emotions on social media can be far more engaging than positive ones. This insight had enormous and unexpected consequences, leading to the rise of clickbait headlines, negative headlines and viral outrage that could incite violence and fuel political polarization. This is a classic example of the "banality of evil." No one at Facebook or other social media companies intended to cause harm, but their sole focus on keeping users attentive and engaged to sell advertising space had unintended and potentially disastrous consequences. And as the AI's inner workings are largely unknown, it's a scary thought that technology has such a powerful influence over our lives.

A recently leaked strategy document from Facebook revealed how advertisers can allegedly target vulnerable teenagers as young as fourteen more effectively with ads by monitoring their posts, images, interactions, and online activities in real-time to determine when they were feeling stressed, anxious, defeated, or overwhelmed. While Facebook claimed the features were only intended to help marketers understand how people express themselves on the platform, the potential for manipulating vulnerable individuals was not denied. As a result, the question of how far companies can and should go in the age of AI to influence others becomes increasingly pressing.

Especially the intersection of advertising and AI has brought about some serious ethical questions about what Cass Sunstein calls the "ethics of influence." AI systems can detect our "prime vulnerability moments" and bombard us with ads for products we're likely to impulsively buy—even if they won't actually make us happy. But what's the harm in that? you ask. Sure, buying another pair of yoga pants you don't need might clutter up your closet, but it's not the end of the world. Well, you should still care because, for starters, manipulators have a sneaky way of getting you to act against your own best interests. Take Facebook's targeted ads aimed at impressionable teenagers, for example. The suspicion is that these ads were designed to exploit moments of weakness and entice them into buying unnecessary products or paying more for them than they should. And it's not just the manipulation itself that's concerning; it's the fact that it's often driven by divergent interests, which should set off alarm bells.

Think about it: if a manipulator had your best interests at heart, why would they need to resort to manipulation in the first place? These "persuasive" strategies may not only rob you of the benefits you deserve, but also distort your consumption patterns and undermine your self-determination. But don't just take our word for it. As consumers become more aware of the manipulative nature of some "persuasive" strategies, there is a growing sense that these tactics are no longer tolerable. So as technology continues to evolve, it is essential that we consider the ethical implications of the ways in which we use it to influence others.

In the world of AI, there's a growing concern about the dangerous potential for manipulation. Today, technology can be easily used to secretly influence our decision-making in many different ways, all with the same end goal: exploiting our vulnerabilities to steer us in a particular direction. As our lives become increasingly intertwined with digital technology, the risk of falling prey to these manipulative practices only grows. With digital surveillance at an all-time high, and AI becoming increasingly powerful, it's easier than ever to identify our weaknesses. And once these vulnerabilities are exposed, digital platforms offer the perfect means to exploit them. With technology playing such a ubiquitous role in our lives, the potential for covert influence is virtually limitless. So in the end, we need to make sure that AI is working with us, not against us. Think of it like this: AI should be like a personal assistant, not a puppet master.

OUR MEMORY IN THE AGE OF CHATGPT: THE GOOGLE EFFECT ON STEROIDS

Imagine you're at a dinner party surrounded by interesting people, engaged in stimulating conversations. You mention a popular movie you saw a few years ago, but for the life of you, you can't recall the name of the lead actor. You try to remember, but it's like a word on the tip of your tongue, just out of reach. You start to feel frustrated. However, before you can dwell on it too much, you pull out your phone, open a search engine, and type in a few keywords. In seconds, you have the answer: Leonardo DiCaprio. The relief is instant, and you feel a sense of satisfaction, not just because you have solved the mystery but also because you have saved yourself from an awkward moment. But have you really used your memory? Or have you simply relied on Google or ChatGPT to do the work for you?

Let's take another example. Imagine you're studying for an exam and you come across a concept you're not familiar with. Remember when you needed to know something and you had to go to the library, open the card catalog, look up the card, pull it out, go upstairs, find the book, hope the book is there, hope nobody tore the page out you need to read, and then tried to understand the concept by reading the book? Nowadays you immediately turn to Google or ChatGPT and search for the concept. In seconds you have access to all the information you need, and you can quickly skim through different sources to find the information that is most relevant to you. You move on to the next concept, and before you know it, you've finished studying. The exam comes, and you feel confident that you know the material. Again, have you really retained the information?

131

Welcome to the digital age, where the line between remembering and Googling is becoming increasingly blurred. A world where it takes no effort to find new information and memories are just a click away. Why strain those tired brain cells when you have Google? With just a click, we have access to all the answers we need, whether it's the lead actor in a movie or how to perform a complicated math trick. Our loyal tech gadgets and AI systems are always there for us, but at what cost?

Google is the king of search engines. With an astounding 3.5 billion queries per day, Google has a monopoly on our search requests. But it's not just Google that allows us to "outsource" our brains; others have joined the ranks as well. For example, Amazon knows our favorite brands and shopping preferences, and Alexa can tell us everything that's on our shopping or to-do lists. It's like these tech giants have become an extension of our own brains. Are we getting dumber as a result? Let's explore how today's support systems are changing the way we process information.

Indeed, Google is changing the way our brains learn. And it's not just search engines that make us rely on our devices for information, it's all the info that's easily accessible on our computers and phones. When it comes to our brain, we've got two types of memory: declarative memory and nondeclarative memory. Declarative memory is responsible for remembering facts, like your phone number or the capital of Switzerland, and events, like your first kiss or the first time you took a plane. This type of memory is processed and stored in the hippocampus and the parahippocampal gyrus. Nondeclarative memory, on the other hand, is responsible for skills, emotions, and movements, like how to ride a bike. This type of memory is processed and stored in different areas of the brain.

When we learn and want to remember things, such as facts or special moments, they must be encoded, stored, and retrieved in the brain. First, the information is encoded into a neural code that can be stored in the brain. In the next step, storage, the encoded information is placed in the hippocampus and the parahippocampal gyrus. In the final step, retrieval, the stored information is ultimately accessed and used from the brain.

But what happens when we have information readily available at all times, and we don't actually need to remember anything? Well, our brain doesn't evolve as quickly as the technologies around us. It still operates in its usual way, encoding, storing, and retrieving stored information. What does change, however, is what we remember. Instead of filling our brains with facts and information, we remember where we can find them. This is called the "Google Effect," a phenomenon that is changing the way we think about memory and how we use it. It's as if we're outsourcing our memory to the internet.

The Google Effect suggests that our constant use of search engines like Google may actually make us more forgetful. The term was coined in 2011 by researchers Betsy Sparrow, Jenny Liu, and Daniel Wegner, who conducted four experiments to investigate the impact of search engines on our memory. In the first experiment, participants were given a list of trivia questions and then had either ten minutes to search for the answers using Google or to retrieve the answers from memory. The results showed that those who used Google to find the answers performed worse on a later memory test for the trivia questions than those who had tried to recall the answers from memory.

In the second experiment, participants were asked to remember a list of words and then given the opportunity to search for the words on Google. The results showed that those who searched for the words on Google had a harder time remembering the words than those who did not search for them.

In the third experiment, participants were presented with a list of trivia questions and then given either ten minutes to search for the answers using Google or asked to recall the answers from memory. After this, they were asked to rate their confidence in their answers. The results showed that those who used Google to find the answers had a higher confidence in their answers, despite performing worse on the subsequent memory test.

And finally, in the fourth experiment a group of participants were asked to read and type forty random facts, like "An ostrich's eye is bigger than its brain" (mind blown, right?!). Half of the participants were told that the facts would be saved on a computer, while the other half were told that the facts would be lost. Then, they were given a memory test to recall the facts they read earlier, and it turns out that the group who were told not to rely on the computer performed better on the test. It's like the brain said, "Oh, I don't have to remember that, it's saved on the computer" and didn't bother to retain it. These results showed that if people believe that the information is saved online and will be accessible at any time, they are less likely to remember that information themselves.

And now what? With the rise of AI, we're going to see the Google effect kick into high gear. AI has led to a shift from the "Information Age" to the "Knowledge Age." The Information Age was all about having access to data and information. Thanks to Google, we could make a search query and the wealth of information was always just a click of a button away. But with the increasing power of AI, we have entered the Knowledge Age. This new era is characterized by the ability to access not just information, but also knowledge. And the key to this shift is AI's ability to make human-like decisions.

AI is increasingly helping us with time-consuming tasks. For example, if we want ideas for healthy and balanced meals for the coming week, until recently, we had to comb through a long list of search results to piece together a suitable meal plan ourselves. But now, we can simply ask You.com or ChatGPT directly for a meal plan tailored to us, and the answer pops right up. Instead of sorting through hundreds of search results, AI can parse through the information, match it with our preferences and requirements, and even summarize it for us. The result is that we don't just receive raw data, but also conclusions, decisions, and ideas—in other words, knowledge.

In the Information Age, we already saw a shift in how we remember things; we turned to Google as a go-to source for easily accessible information. But now, as we enter the Knowledge Age, we'll see an even greater emphasis on outsourcing our memory. After all, we no longer even have to actively "search" for information. Thanks to technological advancements, access to knowledge has become easier than ever before. So the more advanced AI becomes, the more likely the Google Effect will be noticeable.

Offloading our memory is not a new thing. We have always turned to family members, colleagues, or other people to supplement our memory. Just think about how many times you have asked your partner what the new neighbors' names are or your colleague where the next meeting is taking place. This is called the "Group Mind" or transactive memory, and Google is just the latest addition. When we rely on technology, we optimize our memory like a hard drive, remembering where we can find specific information rather than the facts themselves. As our relationship with technology becomes ever closer, retrieving new information is likely to become an increasingly common problem.

Let's test it: Can you call someone in your family on their cell phone without looking up their number? If not, don't worry. Most people are in the same boat. Almost two-thirds of adults can call the landline number of the home they lived in at age ten. But very few know their children's or partner's current phone number. Ultimately, it's not about becoming more forgetful but about using our memory differently to be more efficient.

The Google effect may sound like a bad thing, but some say it's actually a sign of efficiency! Some experts argue that the Google effect is helping us to adapt and thrive in our digital environment and prevents our brain from getting cluttered with unnecessary information. We may not remember certain information because it's so easily accessible online, but that's okay. Because honestly, do you really need to remember that random fact when you can just Google it in seconds? Knowing how and where to find information is sometimes much more valuable than remembering all those nitty-gritty facts, figures, and dates.

But beware! Relying too heavily on technology can impair our cognitive abilities. When we constantly use the internet as a memory aid, we may start to believe that all the information we need is just a click away. But what if that's not the case? Imagine you lose your phone on the go and can't retrieve important information because you never memorized it. Suddenly, you might struggle to find the fastest way home without Google Maps, or you can't inform your family because you don't know their numbers by heart. All at once, you're in a in a tough spot because you have relied too much on technology. The Google Effect can lead to becoming too dependent on technology and getting into trouble when we can no longer access essential information. It's therefore important to maintain a healthy balance between the amount of information we outsource to technology and the information we keep in our own internal storage.

This also applies to images. And here, the Google Effect can even have a negative impact on our well-being and alter our memories. In fact, a study by Linda Henkel, a memory expert, shows that the Google Effect is also applicable to information in the form of images and influences our memories. In the study, two groups of participants went on a museum tour, with one group taking photos of all the museum objects while the other group went through the museum without cameras. After the tour, both groups were questioned about the museum objects. The result: the group with the photos remembered significantly fewer details than the group without cameras and photos.

With the advent of social media and smartphones equipped with professional-grade cameras, we humans snap photos more often than ever before. However, current research indicates that when we take a photo, we're less likely to remember the moment as vividly as if we had just observed it. In other words, living life through the lens of a camera might not be as rich an experience as living it in the moment. So the essence of the story is, instead of just taking a picture, we should take the time to enjoy and appreciate the beautiful moments in life rather than just taking a few photos. Only then will they truly stay with us in the long term.

So what's the best way to navigate digital amnesia? Three simple strategies can improve your memory in the age of AI. First let's talk about the power of being present. Instead of mindlessly scrolling through Google, try to actively seek information. Think of it like a game of "I Spy" for your brain. This will not only improve your memory, but it'll also give you some serious mindfulness points.

Next, it's time to break out the pen and paper. Taking physical notes by hand has been shown to improve memory. In addition, it's a nice break from staring at screens all day. And the act of writing things down helps your brain process the information better.

Finally, let's talk about the elephant in the room: our gadgets. We all know they can be major distractions. So try leaving your tech at home every once in a while. You'll be forced to avoid the temptation of offloading everything and instead remember things without the crutch of Google or ChatGPT. And who knows? You might surprise yourself with how much you can remember!

ON AUTOPILOT: THE RISE OF AI AND THE FALL OF HUMANS?

Becoming a pilot is not for the faint of heart; it takes a unique combination of physical and mental skills to master the art of flying. Pilots must be able to perform complex maneuvers with precision while also making quick calculations and assessments in their heads and all while keeping a vigilant eye on the skies and their surroundings. They must be able to multitask, shifting between manual and cognitive tasks with ease, and remaining focused and alert at all times.

When you first start learning to fly, it can be overwhelming. The controls may seem foreign, and you may have trouble keeping up with the demands of the job. But as you begin to put in the hours of practice and repetition, you start to see progress. The movements become more natural, and you find yourself able to fly with greater precision and less effort. Your brain also starts to adapt, developing mental models that allow you to recognize patterns and respond to situations almost instinctively.

However, with the advent of technology, the nature of the job has changed, and computers have taken on an increasing number of tasks that were previously performed by pilots. One example is the automatic flight control system (AFCS), which can automatically control the aircraft's altitude, speed, and heading, relieving the pilot of the need to manually make adjustments. Modern aircrafts are equipped with fly-by-wire (FBW) technology, which is comparable to having a super intelligent copilot who's always looking out for you. Instead of the traditional mechanical controls, FBW uses cutting-edge computer technology to process your flight commands and make sure the aircraft is doing exactly what you want it to do. With FBW you're no longer directly connected to the aircraft's control surfaces; instead, your inputs are read by a computer that makes sure everything is running smoothly. Another example is the navigation system, which can automatically calculate the best route and flight plan, reducing the pilot's workload. Additionally, modern aircraft are equipped with a variety of advanced sensors and systems that can detect and diagnose potential problems, alerting the pilot to any potential issues.

So here it is, the future of flying! With all the shiny gadgets and gizmos in the cockpit, pilots can kick back, relax, and let the machines do the heavy lifting, leaving them free to focus on the important stuff, such as keeping the plane on course, chatting with the control tower, and making life-saving decisions in case of an emergency. But here's the catch: all this automation can also be a double-edged sword. You see, when pilots don't have to do as much work, they don't practice as much, which can make them less proficient at flying the old-fashioned way. It's like a video game; when the game is too easy, you don't get better at it. This can be a problem when an emergency strikes and the pilots need to take the wheel, but they're not as skilled as they could be.

This downside of computers taking over is called "deskilling." In other words, the lack of practice and experience in manual flying can make pilots less proficient in handling the aircraft in emergency situations, which is a concern for safety. Thus, while computers are making flying easier, they also pose a risk of pilots becoming less skilled in the manual operation of the aircraft, and this raises an issue of balancing the need for efficient automation with the need for maintaining the pilot's skill set.

Unfortunately, deskilling can have catastrophic consequences. On May 31, 2009, the world was shaken by the tragic crash of an Air France Airbus A330. This state-of-the-art aircraft, with 228 passengers on board, had taken off from Rio de Janeiro bound for Paris. However, three hours into the flight, the jet encountered a severe storm over the Atlantic. The storm had a catastrophic effect on the plane's air-speed sensors, causing them to become caked with ice and giving faulty readings. This caused the autopilot to disengage and put the fate of the aircraft and its passengers solely in the hands of the two expert pilots.

As a later reconnaissance revealed, a series of fundamental mistakes were made when control of the aircraft was handed over to the pilots. As soon as the autopilot shut off, the warning system inside the cockpit began to sound, indicating that the plane was at risk of stalling. This means that the plane was losing its speed and beginning to fall. Pilots are trained to react to this situation by pushing the control stick forward, causing the plane to go downward and pick up speed, allowing it to counteract the stall and regain altitude. However, the expert pilots did the exact opposite and pulled back on the stick, which lifted the plane's nose and slowed it down even more. This continued for several minutes as all kinds of warnings blared in the cockpit while the plane rapidly fell into a stall, lost altitude, and plummeted thirty thousand feet in just three minutes. The crash resulted in the deaths of all 228 passengers on board.

The French investigators later said that the pilots showed a "total loss of cognitive control over the situation," which ultimately resulted in the crash. Unfortunately, this was not an isolated incident. While the total number of airplane crashes decreases, the number of airplane crashes caused by pilots becoming too dependent on computerized systems has been on the rise. In 2013, the Federal Aviation Administration (FAA) released a safety alert notice to all US airlines and other commercial air carriers, warning them of the dangers of overreliance on technology and encouraging them to promote manual flight operations. The FAA had collected evidence from crash investigations, incident reports, and cockpit studies indicating that pilots had become too dependent on computerized systems. This overuse can lead to a decline in their ability to quickly recover the aircraft from an undesired state. Thus it concluded with the recommendation that airlines, as a matter of operational policy, should instruct pilots to spend less time flying on autopilot and more time flying by hand.

This tragic incident serves as a powerful reminder that we must all stay vigilant and continue to develop our skills even as technology becomes more prevalent in our lives. This is not just a problem for pilots, but also a concern for all of us. It's happening to you, too. Can you remember when you last wrote a letter without the help of programs such as grammar and spell checkers? And do you remember the phone numbers of even your closest friends and family, or do you just pull them up on your phone? What was the last exciting adventure you embarked on where you ditched the digital and relied on a good old-fashioned physical map to plan your journey to a specific destination?

Take another example of simple calculations. Remember the days when math was a struggle and calculations were done with pen and paper? With lots of repetition and practice, we learned to master it. But now calculators have made it a piece of cake. Just a tap of a button and voilà! Even the most complex math problem is solved. But this ease of use has made us forget our own mathematical abilities; even simple calculations can seem hard because we're out of practice from solving them mentally. So you see, technologically induced deskilling already happens in our everyday life.

Deskilling occurs when we rely too heavily on AI to perform tasks for us, to the point where we are no longer practicing and improving our own skills. For example, journalist

John Seabrook found that his use of Google's Smart Compose tool was impacting his own writing skills. After starting a sentence with "I am p . . ." and allowing Smart Compose to complete it with "I am proud of you," Seabrook realized that he had surrendered control to the machine. He wondered if he was allowing AI to become his cowriter and if it was a step backward for his own writing abilities. Many of us have similar experiences when using AI in our daily lives. When we rely too much on these tools, we can become too passive, not putting in the effort to improve our own skills and abilities. Alarmingly, this can lead to a "satisficing tendency" in which we settle for a result that is just good enough.

As AI is increasingly able to perform more complex tasks and enters the domain of knowledge workers, the same thing can happen for more intricate areas. And this is where things get really critical! The more difficult the tasks are, the more crucial it becomes to have adequate training and practice, as machine failures can lead to more serious consequences. The aviation industry is a prime example of that. So exploring the impact of automation on the aviation industry can provide a glimpse into the future of how machines will continue to shape our world. This is because the aviation industry was one of the first industries that aggressively tried to find ways to shift work from people to machines, leading to the early and widespread adoption of computer systems, many of them powered by AI. What the aviation industry did decades ago, other industries are doing now, incorporating similar computer systems to improve their processes and operations. The question arising is that as technology continues to advance, how will it affect other sectors and society as a whole?

Let's look at two examples where AI is currently taking over the domain.

The medical field is seeing a growing influence of AI in areas such as ophthalmology, radiology, molecular medicine, and pediatric care. While previously, doctors would rely on their physical examination skills, visual perception, and cognitive abilities to make a diagnosis and plan of treatment, now there are automatic screening and decision-aid systems based on deep learning that are becoming more prevalent. Given our prior discussion, it may not come as a surprise that there are concerns that doctors may lose their clinical skills and become too reliant on AI recommendations. This can lead to decreased ability to make informed decisions, inaccuracies in identifying pathologies, and decreased confidence in their own abilities.

Imagine a world where surgeries are performed entirely by machines, with robotic arms guided by advanced algorithms. These robots can move with precision and speed that exceeds the capabilities of human hands, making surgeries less invasive and more efficient. But what happens when something goes wrong and the robot malfunctions? The surgeon must be able to take over the surgery by hand, but if they haven't been practicing that skill, they may not be as proficient.

Self-driving cars are another example. These cars are equipped with a host of sensors and cameras that allow them to navigate the roads on their own. They can change lanes, avoid obstacles, and even park themselves. As a result of advancing technology, the skill levels needed to drive a car decrease. The human's role shifts from active engagement to mere monitoring, which raises the potential for loss of manual driving skills. But what happens if something goes wrong and the driver needs to take over? This is why many self-driving cars still have steering wheels and pedals so the driver can take over when the problem is still too complex for the intelligent system. However, if you haven't driven a car in a while, you may not be as comfortable behind the wheel. It's like skiing; if you don't do it for a while, you may feel rather shaky and uneasy on your feet.

And deskilling isn't the only problem in these cases. Just picture this: You're sitting in a self-driving car, enjoying your favorite music, and feeling like a boss. The car is running smoothly, and you're not even touching the steering wheel. But, as you're lost in your own world, the car starts to malfunction, and you don't even notice. Why? Because you've fallen victim to automation complacency. Automation complacency is a fancy term for when you get too comfortable with automation technology and start to trust it blindly. You assume everything is under control, even when the system malfunctions. You become a little too reliant on technology and stop paying attention to what's going on around you.

And it's not just limited to self-driving cars. It can happen with any AI-enabled automation technology. Pilots, air traffic controllers, and even doctors who rely too heavily on AI may suffer from automation complacency. Due to overconfidence in technology, we humans can overlook critical situations in our professional and private lives, which can lead to accidents or mistakes.

A related issue is the so-called automation bias. This is when you trust the recommendations of an automated system so much that you stop thinking critically. You assume that the technology knows better and blindly follow its advice. The problem is, even the most advanced technology can get it wrong sometimes. ChatGPT, for example, can "hallucinate" every once in a while, and invent sources and articles that don't even exist but sound credible. But there may be even more dangerous omission or commission errors when technology fails. Just think of the number of GPS-related accidents. These have been on the rise for years.

In some cases, drivers have followed their GPS instructions blindly, even when it led them into dangerous or incorrect situations. The tourists who drove their car into the ocean trying to reach an Australian island is a prime example of this.

They followed the GPS instructions, only to realize too late that they were driving off a cliff. In their own words, "It kept saying it would navigate us to a road." Ultimately, blindly delegating all tasks to technology and fully entrusting it to do our job can make us lose control over the situation if we don't stay smart and are no longer up for the task ourselves.

So what's the solution? It's crucial to keep in mind the dangers of losing control to AI and essential to understand the factors that lead to overreliance on AI and how to counter them. By being mindful of this, we can ensure that we avoid the negative consequences that can come from blindly following instructions from AI.

As technology continues to advance at a rapid pace, it's up to each of us, as well as our educational systems and organizations, to make sure we don't lose our skills in the process. We must proactively take measures to prevent the de-skilling of people in the era of AI. Only in this way can we ensure that we keep up with the constantly evolving technological landscape and that these tools make us better, not worse.

But even when the human is retained as a backup to AI-enabled automation, they need to be vigilant and not get too complacent. The key is finding the right balance between human judgment and automation technology.

As individuals, it's up to us to stay sharp and prevent ourselves from losing our skills. One way to do this is by using our own judgment first, and then double-checking our findings with the latest technology. For example, a doctor should trust their own physical examination before turning to AI for guidance. Additionally, to make informed decisions it's important for us to have a conceptual understanding of how algorithms work.

When it comes to education, it's crucial that we don't let certain essential skills fall by the wayside, no matter how advanced AI gets. These core abilities should be defined and built into our educational and training programs, even if they're not used as frequently in everyday life. For instance, doctors should always be able to examine the eye and spot certain diseases, and surgeons should be able to perform surgeries without relying on technology. It may seem unnecessary now, but aviation history has shown us that if we're not careful, these skills can quickly become things of the past.

And finally, it's essential that organizations take proactive steps to prevent deskilling and to promote responsible AI implementation. So what's the secret sauce? It's called "hybrid intelligence" and it's all about bringing together the best of both worlds—humans and AI. Think of it like a superhero duo—Batman and Robin, if you will. Together they can tackle any problem that comes their way! Instead of just relying on technology to do all the heavy lifting, we need to find ways to combine human expertise with AI power to create sustainable solutions. By using hybrid intelligence, we can enhance our skills and capabilities rather than diminish them.

In conclusion, while automation technology can make our lives easier, it's crucial to remain alert and not let it run on autopilot. As with an escalator, we can comfortably stand still and let it carry us upwards, but that makes us unfit in the long run. If we move along with technology, we'll be faster than before. What applies to our motor skills also applies to our cognitive abilities. We must not rest on technology. As the saying goes, "If you don't use it, you'll lose it!" So stay alert, stay sharp, stay up-to-date! Because the reality is, technology is only going to continue to advance, and it's up to us to ensure that we're using it to benefit everyone.

IS AI TURNING US INTO MACHINES? THE DEHUMANIZING EFFECTS OF AI COMPANIONS

Imagine a world where robots and AI are so advanced, they are our constant companions, helping us with our daily tasks and even becoming part of our social circles. But what happens to the way we connect and interact with each other?

According to MIT professor and pioneer in the field Sherry Turkle, technology can diminish our emotional lives. In today's hyperconnected world, it's easy to fall into the trap of thinking that online relationships can replace face-to-face communication. With the ability to amass thousands of Twitter and Facebook friends, we often mistake tweets and likes for genuine connections. However, this constant connectivity can actually lead to a sense of loneliness and disconnection. Turkle's research is among the first to uncover the unsettling changes in relationships between and among friends, lovers, and families that have resulted from our reliance on technology. Through hundreds of interviews, she finds how it harms our ability to form authentic connections, ultimately leading us to be what she calls "alone together."

But this is just the start. Consider a future where AI has evolved to the point where it's not just a tool but also a companion. What happens when our interactions are no longer just with fellow humans, but increasingly with our artificially intelligent companions? How will this affect our social skills and the way we connect and interact with each other?

The more we rely on machines, the less we interact with actual human beings. And that's where the trouble starts. We become more independent, but also lonelier and less empathic toward others. What's even scarier is that we might start seeing people as less than fully human. That's called dehumanization, and it's shockingly commonplace and consequential.

While there hasn't been direct research on dehumanization, social psychologist Adam Waytz—author of the book The Power of Human—argues that a variety of related trends indicate its increase. People are lonelier, less trusting, and less connected to their communities than in the past. Furthermore, empathy has declined between 1979 and 2009. The decline suggests that something has changed in how we interact with others.

Today, AI is changing the game. It's revolutionizing the way we interact with our devices, and more importantly, with each other. As digital assistants become more prevalent, we're starting to treat them like real-life confidants, friends, and even therapists. But the big question is what happens to our human relationships as we grow more comfortable talking to our devices like they're living, breathing beings?

Well, the truth is, we're already seeing the effects of AI on our social lives and ways in which it transforms accepted approaches to social interactions. For example, parents are concerned that their children's lack of manners toward digital assistants such as Alexa or Siri could bleed into how they treat people. And indeed, children who grow up relating to AI instead of to humans may struggle to develop empathy and establish meaningful connections.

But what about human cooperation? Cooperation is essential to human society; it's what helps us work together toward common goals and create successful communities. But recent research from Yale suggests that our relationship with AI could throw a wrench in the works. In a fascinating experiment, the researchers investigated how AI influences the "tragedy of the commons"—the idea that when individuals act in their own self-interests, it can result in collective harm.

Several thousands of participants were given money to use in an online game that consisted of multiple rounds. At the start of each round, participants could choose to keep the money for themselves or donate some or all of it to their neighbors. If they chose to donate, the experimenters would match the amount, doubling the money that their neighbors received.

At first, two thirds of players acted altruistically and donated to their neighbors, understanding that their generosity in one round could be reciprocated by their neighbor in the next. Clearly, from a selfish and short-term perspective, the best outcome would have been to keep the money for themselves and receive money from their neighbors. To test how AI might affect participants' cooperation and generosity, a few selfish bots were added to the mix.

What happened when these bots were present? It's sad to say, but the human players began to follow suit, and eventually, everyone stopped cooperating altogether. The bots had converted a group of generous people into a group of egomaniacs. The study has shown that adding AI to our social environment can lead us to become less productive and less ethical.

Let's think for a moment about what this discovery means for us. Cooperation makes our social life go 'round. Trust and being generous set successful groups apart from not-so-successful ones. When we all pitch in and make sacrifices for the greater good, everyone wins. But when that cooperation breaks down, goodbye public good and hello suffering for all. And the idea that AI could potentially mess with our ability to work together is distressing.

Fortunately, researchers are already working on how AI can improve our collaboration, not make it worse. In another experiment at the same lab at Yale, researchers had small groups of people and a blue-and-white humanoid robot sitting around a table, using tablets to work on laying virtual railroad tracks. The robot was programmed to make mistakes and to recognize them, saying, "Sorry, guys, I made the mistake this round. I know it may be hard to believe, but even robots make mistakes."

Results showed that amazingly, this clumsy, apologetic robot actually helped the groups do better by boosting communication among the humans. They became more relaxed and conversational, offering help to those who stumbled and laughing together more often than the control groups, who had a robot that only said bland comments.

And let's look at one last experiment, where four thousand participants were split into groups of about twenty. Each person was assigned individual "friends" within the group, which formed their social network. The task was simple: pick one of three colors, but none of your "virtual friends" could have the same color as you.

Little did the participants know that some groups had sneaky little bots mixed in, programmed to make mistakes on purpose. And guess what? The humans who were directly connected to these bots became super flexible and avoided getting stuck in a solution that worked for just them but not for the group as a whole. And that flexibility spread throughout the whole network, even to those who weren't directly connected to the bots. As a result, the groups with mistake-prone bots outdid the groups without them. The bots helped the humans help themselves. Who knew?

This suggests that AI technology isn't all negative. These studies show that when humans and robots mingle and form "hybrid systems," the right kind of AI can make us all get along better. And it's not just these studies; there are others that offer hope. For example, political scientist Kevin Munger has programmed a bot to crack down on people who were sending racist stuff to others online. He found that under certain conditions, a bot that simply reminded the sender that the person on the receiving end is a human being with feelings, can make that person stop using racist language for more than a month. Good news, right?

Ultimately, the rapid development of AI raises important questions: How does it affect our interpersonal relationships? Can we continue to build profound and meaningful connections with others? There's a chance that AI might make it harder for us to form deep connections with others and that it might make our relationships less meaningful, superficial, or more self-centered. We need to be aware of how AI might affect our emotional well-being and how we can prepare for it.

In the past, our innate capacities for love, friendship, cooperation, and teaching have helped us live together as a community. But we don't have time to evolve new innate capacities to live with robots, so we need to make sure they can live peacefully with us. As AI becomes more integrated into our lives, we may need a new social contract, one with machines instead of with other humans.

CHAPTER 5

FEEDING AI: WHY YOUR DATA IS THE NEW HAPPY MEAL FOR AI

As we continue to integrate artificial intelligence into our daily lives, we are also giving AI access to vast amounts of our personal data. From the way we speak and type, to our search history and location data, AI is collecting information about us at an unprecedented rate. But what does this mean for us?

As we delve deeper into this chapter, we will explore the aspect of AI and Big Data and how it can make us feel like we're living in a dystopian novel. But before we get there, let's first remember what AI is and how it works. Essentially, AI mimics human intelligence. This is why AI is often referred to as a "machine that simulates the human mind." It's why we have things such as self-driving cars, computer programs that can beat humans in complex games, and personal assistants such as Siri. But here's the catch: AI is nothing without data. It needs data to learn from, to become smarter and more efficient. As we'll see later, this is where the spooky side of AI comes in. So buckle up and let's see how your data is the new happy meal for AI!

THE INTERNET: A GIANT BUFFET FOR GENERATIVE AI?

Imagine a giant buffet filled with all sorts of delicious dishes—from spicy curries to sweet desserts. Now imagine that instead of food, this buffet is filled with data. Welcome to the internet, where generative AI has found a never-ending source of information to feast on!

Generative AI, or creative AI, is like a wizard that can conjure up new and original content, like in music, art, text, and even video. How does it do it? By training on vast amounts of data and learning patterns that it can use to create similar content. As you can imagine, creating such a generative AI model is a complex and resource-intensive task that requires significant amounts of data, funding, and expertise. So far, only a few large technology companies such as OpenAI, Deep-Mind, and Meta have been able to successfully develop and release generative AI models.

To illustrate the size of generative AI models, we can take OpenAI's ChatGPT-3 as an example. It was trained on 45 terabytes of data and uses an astounding 175 billion parameters to make its predictions; its successor, GPT-4, is set to reach an astronomical 100 trillion parameters, a staggering 600 times more than its predecessor.

Training such models can be very expensive, especially when using vast amounts of data that practically map the entire internet: estimates suggest that a single training run for GPT-3 costs $12 million. Fortunately, large companies like OpenAI have received billions of dollars in funding to train such models. Others, however, are not so lucky.

Smaller companies and individuals struggle to raise such resources, creating high barriers to entry. But there is hope: in the future, large technology companies could train extensive AI models and then make them accessible to other businesses and individuals through an application programming interface (API). This could become an essential part of future technology infrastructure.

But where do generative AI models actually get this data? You guessed it: the internet! With billions of users and devices connected to it, the internet is a constantly evolving landscape that provides an endless supply of data for generative AI to learn from. From social media posts to online articles, images to videos, the internet is a treasure trove of information that fuels the advancements in the field of AI. It's like a giant buffet of images and texts that these models can learn from.

But as with any buffet, you have to be careful about what you put on your plate. With so much data available, it can be tricky to find the right information to train on and to filter out the bad stuff. And sometimes the quality of the data can vary greatly, which can impact the accuracy and effectiveness of the generative AI models. Many also just help themselves without asking and are trained on copyrighted data. This could mean big trouble for copyright and those who hold the rights to the works being used. For example, Microsoft-owned GitHub Copilot, based on OpenAI's Codex model, is currently facing a lawsuit claiming it was built on "mega software piracy." Apparently, the system was trained on code scraped from the web, which may have licenses that require giving credit to the original creators when using their code. Other generative AI models face similar criticisms when using others' work to train these models. So the use of the internet as a resource raises concerns around copyright issues, data privacy, and the potential for biased or harmful content.

Some artists are worried that their work will be used to train AI algorithms. They want assurances that their art won't be used in this way and don't want their names to be used as prompts for AI-generated art. For example, one of the most popular prompts in the Stable Diffusion generator is fantasy landscape artist Greg Rutkowski. In fact, his name has been used ninety-three thousand times already—more often than famous artists such as Picasso! However, Greg isn't exactly jumping for joy about this newfound popularity. He feels like his livelihood is being threatened and he never gave permission for his work to be used in this way. But, like all attempts at censorship, this is easy to circumvent. You can spell the name differently or just describe the style in words. And even if an artist's name is off-limits, their influence will still be present.

In response, technological solutions are being developed to address these issues. For example, researchers at the University of Chicago—and clearly some big Harry Potter fans—have developed a tool that adds a cloak of invisibility to images to stop AI models from learning an artist's style. Humans, of course, cannot see this invisibility cloak. But it disables the AI to learn from the artist's image. This can help art creators protect their work and ensure it is not used unwantedly by generative AI models.

Another concern for artists is that big corporations will make money off their work without compensating them. After all, open-source programs such as Stable Diffusion or DALL-E are built by scraping images from the internet without attribution to the artists. So many suggest that in the future, the art sector may shift toward a pay-per-play or subscription model like the film and music industries.

There are ideas, however, about how to treat and compensate creators more fairly. One idea would be to compensate artists based on the frequency their work is referenced in commercial text-to-image applications. This is similar to the economic models used in music streaming, and could be a step toward ensuring that artists are properly recognized and rewarded for their hard work. While there is no perfect solution yet, it is important that we start thinking about how we can protect and support artists and their work today as we embrace new technologies like AI and generative models.

At the moment, the question of whether this type of training is considered plagiarism is still unresolved and could take many years, or even decades, to be resolved. However, it is important to remember that the idea of generative AI models is to build new art. They learned from prior work, just like a human artist may learn from and is influenced by Picasso or Van Gogh. And society doesn't expect human artists to pay other human artists for their influence on their work. So it seems unlikely that AI algorithms will be expected to pay their influencers. The "tax" that successful artists pay for their success is their unpaid influence on the success of others.

There is an exception, however. If these models simply ruminate copies of copyrighted artwork—as recent research suggests—then this becomes a whole different story. There are already some companies and art creators who are working to ensure that AI-generated art is labeled and clearly separated from "real" art. For example, Getty Images, a leading agency for stock photos and illustrations, has already banned AI-generated images. In a similar vein, some artists on DeviantArt have also called for a ban.

Generative AI can be used to create new images, texts, or videos by learning from previous works. Just as an artist learns from and is influenced by others, AI algorithms are influenced by the works they learn from. Even if individual artists demand that their artwork be removed from the training data, you should know this: with billions of images in the training dataset, one person's artwork doesn't play a significant role. The influence of famous artists remains, whether their images are included in the training data or not. Imagine if we removed all of Van Gogh's paintings from the training data. His style would still be present in other works that were influenced by his style. This highlights the importance of considering the copyright and ownership of the works being used to train these models. It is safe to say that this discussion is far from over. And it highlights that it's important to remember that there are real people behind the works being used to train these models and to approach the development and use of AI in art with care and responsibility!

Generative AI is a total game-changer in many aspects and tasks. But considering its huge impact and the barriers to entry, it's important to handle its spread in and effect on society and the economy with care. There are concerns around the disruption of the job market, data privacy, licensing, copyright issues, and the potential for biased or even harmful content, fake news, and more. But don't let that scare you away! The potential benefits of using the internet as a data source for generative AI are enormous. By harnessing the power of the internet, generative AI can create new and exciting content that is both original and relevant to current trends and events.

DON'T THINK YOUR FACEBOOK LIKES ARE INTERESTING? THINK AGAIN

Here's a little story about Liam. Liam writes computer programs and is well-versed in code and algorithms. But lately, she's been feeling uneasy because there's a lot of personal information about her on the internet. She thinks that companies know too much about her, and that worries her. What concerns Liam the most is the fact that her smartphone constantly records her location as she carries it around. But she's sure that's not all: when she reviews a pizzeria on Google, or leaves a comment on her local newspaper's website, that becomes part of her digital profile. Advertisers then use this information to possibly persuade her to buy things, support certain opinions, or vote for someone. There's simply a ton of data about her, and most of it is free for the taking.

One day, after shopping at a hardware store, Liam receives an email from the company asking about her visit. Liam is pretty sure the company used the location tracking on her work phone to find her. This is all too much for Liam; she feels that her personal data is being collected by so-called data brokers—companies that collect and sell data about people, including personal information, online behavior, and purchasing habits, to third parties— and that social media is helping them target advertising at her.

Liam decides that enough is enough, and she plans to take control of her personal information. She quits most social media accounts and switches to a search engine that promises to protect her privacy. Liam also cleans up her smartphone, removing all "app crap" while trying to reclaim as much of her personal data as possible from data dealers. She even pays for a service called DeleteMe, which helps people erase information from databases. She wants to get as much information off the internet as possible. Liam isn't against technology; she just wants to have control over her own data. And she is not alone in this; 86 percent of US citizens have already attempted to delete or decrease the information about them on the internet. Many people are concerned about what data is collected about them, who has access to it, and how it's used. But is this fear justified? Or are people such as Liam overly concerned?

Unfortunately, Liam's concern is valid and refers to the traces of data that we leave behind when using the internet and digital devices, known as a "digital footprint." Imagine you're on a digital adventure, just like Liam, and with each website you visit, app you use, and form you fill out, you're leaving behind a little digital treasure. This includes the websites you visit, search queries, apps you use, locations, and even personal information like your name and address. These can be collected, analyzed, and used to create a profile of you. When all of these treasures, or bits of information, are pieced together, they can create a detailed picture of who you are and what you do online.

But here's the problem: unlike a real hike, the digital forest is filled with all sorts of creatures, some of them not so friendly. Advertisers, scammers, and even cybercriminals are lurking around every corner, looking to use your digital footprint to target you with ads, steal your identity, or commit fraud. Small, questionably legitimate data farmers are likely scraping social media as well as buying stolen consumer data off the dark web. Worse, cybercriminals and extremist groups have used these methods. A few years ago, members of the alt-right—a loose collection of neo-Nazis and white supremacists—attempted to create data profiles of supposed far-left activists with the intent of using the data to harass them. Unfortunately, those groups have a lot of data to work with these days.

We have all unwittingly become "data creators." The digital footprint we all leave online goes well beyond sharing photos and messages on Facebook. In fact, when we surf online, we leave two different footprints: those where we take action ourselves, and those that are created in the background without us doing anything.

A passive digital footprint is created without our knowledge or active participation. This type of footprint is created when information is gathered about our online activities through browsing history, search queries, and online purchases. This information is collected by websites, search engines, and third-party companies, often for targeted advertising or data analytics. But it doesn't stop right there in front of our computers. Retailers may also use facial recognition technology in their stores, where your image is being captured and analyzed. Similarly, the use of smart home devices such as iRobot Roomba can create detailed maps of your home.

On the other hand, an active digital footprint refers to the digital trail that we intentionally create by actively sharing or posting content online, such as social media posts, comments, and blog articles. This type of footprint is created by our own actions and can be easily controlled by adjusting privacy settings, deleting content, or simply refraining from posting anything in the first place.

You might think that only big tech companies such as Google or intelligence agencies like the NSA can access your personal data, but think again. It's also that innocent looking game on your phone that just got access to the history of your location data. With the advancement of technology, more and more devices and services are becoming connected to the internet, causing our digital footprint to expand and evolve. The internet is becoming deeply ingrained in our daily lives, and as a result we are generating more data than ever before. In fact, almost everyone who has ever used the internet has some sort of online footprint. Today, there are nearly 5 billion internet users worldwide.

The rise of social networks has greatly impacted our digital footprint. Social media platforms have turned the internet into a much more interactive place, where people are not just reading but also commenting, sharing, and liking. This has made it easier for people to create an online persona with minimal technical skill, and as a result huge amounts of personal data are being shared online. Currently there are 4.62 billion active social media users, and the number continues to grow at an astonishing rate of almost 13.5 new users per second.

The coronavirus pandemic has only increased the amount of personal data online because more people turned to the internet for work, school, and social connections. The number of pieces of online personally identifiable information per individual has jumped 150 percent in the past two years, boosted by increases in both data broker activity and pandemic-related consumer screen time.

Every online activity, from Google searches to Facebook likes and Amazon purchases, adds to our digital footprint. This has led to an unprecedented amount of behavioral, preference, and demographic data on hundreds of millions of people. There's a wide number of organizations collecting and storing your data. And it's not just sitting there collecting dust, it's being traded on huge online marketplaces, where anyone can buy your intimate information for just a few cents. As data brokers are still largely unregulated, understanding how our data is used and by whom can feel like a losing game.

The advancement of technology has not only increased the amount of data available and created, but it has also expanded the possibilities of what can be done with the data. Creating massive databases of consumer profiles has gotten as easy as pie, thanks to the magic of artificial intelligence technology that allows for better cross-referencing and correcting of data. The databases are bigger and more accurate than ever, allowing detailed profiles of people based on various digital traces. These include info about behavior, preferences, and even personality traits.

The more behavioral data is collected in real time, the better the psychological characteristics of people in different situations can be assessed. For example, people's mood and emotions can be successfully inferred from spoken and written language, video, or wearable devices and smartphone sensor data. This information can be used to identify critical time periods for psychological persuasion. After all, people in a good mood are more inclined to make impulse purchases.

These predictions can be done with high accuracy through the use of AI and machine learning algorithms that can analyze and extract powerful insights from seemingly uninteresting pieces of data. However, it also means that sensitive information that a person may not want to share can also be uncovered.

For example, a study found that Facebook likes can be used to predict a wide range of characteristics of Facebook users, such as sexual orientation, ethnicity, religious and political views, personality traits, intelligence, happiness, use of addictive substances, parental separation, age, and gender. And it's not as straightforward as you would expect. AI models can use seemingly insignificant information, such as what you've liked on social media, to predict certain traits or characteristics about you that may not have any direct correlation to the content of what you've liked.

Let's illustrate this last point. Do you like curly fries? And even more importantly, would you share this information on social media? If you are like most people, you wouldn't mind much about sharing such a trivial piece of information about yourself. But what if we told you that this piece of information reflects so much more about yourself than your taste buds?

Indeed, researchers have recently discovered that by analyzing our digital data, such as our Facebook likes, they can predict all sorts of private things about us, including our personality traits and even our level of intelligence. And one of the strongest indicators of high intelligence, according to the study, is liking curly fries! Clearly, you may be wondering "How can my love for those delicious, curly, golden fries be a sign of my superior intellect?"

It's not about the fries themselves, it's about the underlying theories behind how information spreads through social networks. The study found that things such as Facebook likes spread in the same way that diseases spread through social networks. For example, an intelligent person might have liked curly fries, which then led to smart people in their close circle of friends also liking it, and so on. Liking curly fries is not directly related to intelligence. Instead, it shows that people with similar characteristics—in this case, high intelligence—tend to like similar content. So if a person with high intelligence likes curly fries on Facebook, it's likely that their clever friends (who also share similar traits) will like the page too. This results in the liking of curly fries being indirectly associated with high intelligence, as it reflects a common characteristic of the people who like this page. It's important to note that this is not a direct cause-and-effect relationship. Rather, it demonstrates that people with similar traits tend to like similar things and behave similarly in social networks.

Thanks to the work of experts in the field, we now know that AI can accurately predict not only our intelligence, but also our personality, political views and sexual orientation, just by analyzing our Facebook likes. Facebook likes used to be publicly available online and – as we now know at the least since this study – posed a significant privacy risk. After the publication of the article about how Facebook likes can lead to privacy risks, Facebook took action and tightened its privacy rules, and likes became private by default. But for many, the damage was already done, as companies such as Cambridge Analytica had already collected enough data to invade the privacy of millions of people.

However, it's not just Facebook likes that can be used to extract intimate information. Even a person's profile picture can reveal a wealth of personal details, thanks to the power of modern facial recognition algorithms. By analyzing various aspects of a person's profile picture, such as their posture, make-up, hairstyle, and facial expressions, modern facial recognition algorithms can extract a wealth of intimate information about a person, including their personality and political orientation. And all this is just the tip of the iceberg when it comes to the data that can be collected and analyzed. Just think about all the information that can be extracted from search keywords, online clicks, posts, and reviews.

In short, every time you scroll through your Facebook feed, like a tweet, or post a picture on Instagram, you're leaving behind a digital footprint. Remember that these digital footprints can reveal a lot about you, from your personality to your moods and emotions. This means that advertisers and even governments can use this information to influence your behavior, whether it's in your best interests or not.

For example, imagine that you're scrolling through your Facebook feed one day and you see an advertisement for a new gambling app. It's targeted to you because AI has analyzed your digital footprint and determined that you have a higher likelihood of falling for a persuasive pitch. Or maybe you're in a good mood and you're more susceptible to impulse buys, so you see an ad for a product you've been eyeing for a while.

While not everyone is trying to trick you into things you don't want, one thing is for sure: the more data that is collected, the more accurate these predictions will become and the more powerful the tool of psychological mass persuasion will be. So the next time you post that cute cat picture on Instagram or like that meme on Twitter, remember that you're leaving behind a digital footprint that can reveal a lot about you.

So how can we take back control of our own data and privacy? Sure, you could throw your smartphone out the window, cancel your internet service, and delete all your social media accounts. But those things are not exactly practical or fun. Plus, the data that tech companies and advertisers have collected on you would still exist, lurking in the background. Instead of trying to erase your digital footprint entirely, you can take steps to minimize it. Here are a few simple ways to protect your data and keep it out of shady hands:

1. Think twice about what you post. Don't share posts that can impact your online reputation and avoid sharing personally identifiable information such as your email address, mailing address, phone number, bank information, and ID numbers such as your Social Security number, driver's license, and passport.

2. Adjust your privacy settings. Limit who can see your posts and better protect your online presence, but remember that the settings don't guarantee privacy.

3. Consider privacy trade-offs of new apps and accounts. Think about the data cost before signing up for new apps or accounts, and weigh the benefits against the personal data they will collect.

4. Delete old apps and accounts. This will prevent companies from collecting more data about you and it will also reduce the chances of cybercriminals taking over your old accounts and using them for fraudulent activities.

In the end, however, collecting and using our personal data is a two-way street. It's important for you to be aware of the data that's being collected and how it's being used. It's also important to advocate for laws that protect our data and privacy. But it is also important for companies and organizations to be transparent about their practices and respect our rights to our own data. Together we can ensure that our digital friendship with AI is a healthy and mutually beneficial one.

TO SHARE OR NOT TO SHARE? ON THE PERSONALIZATION-PRIVACY PARADOX

After reading about all this data that is collected and the information that can be drawn about you, you may wonder WHY? Why do you put up with all of this?

Well, the answer is simple: if we surrender our data to AI, only then can it really serve and support us. For example, if you have the Google Photos App installed, you allow Google to capture your personal pictures. But in return, you get AI-powered photo albums featuring your favorite time-out in the mountains or the yummiest desserts you have had in 2022. So yes, companies can use our data and feed it to AI to create the most personalized experience for us possible.

The benefits of data and AI go beyond just convenience and personalization. As we share more of our personal information with companies, we can also have a better online experience that is tailored to our interests and preferences. This can lead to more relevant ads, recommendations, and even discounts. For example, by providing our browsing history and search preferences, online retailers can suggest products that we may be interested in and offer personalized deals. Similarly, streaming services such as Netflix and Spotify can use our viewing and listening history to recommend content that aligns with our preferences. So don't be surprised to get Harry and Meghan as the top recommendation on Netflix after binge-watching the full Crown series. The idea behind this recommendation is not only to make your Netflix experience more enjoyable, but also to save you time and effort in finding the next content to watch.

But this isn't all. Have you ever wondered how credit card companies are able to detect and prevent fraud? Again, the answer lies in the power of the data that AI collects and learns about you. By providing companies with our personal information, they can use machine learning algorithms to analyze patterns of behavior, such as our typical credit card usage, to detect suspicious and unusual activities and prevent fraud. This can protect both the credit card company and the customer from financial loss. So next time you receive an email or call, asking if this was really you logging in from a new device or spending that much money in Dubai, don't get annoyed by it. Just remember, this is probably an AI system trying to keep you secure!

But there is a fine line between intimacy and intrusion that companies need to manage. Too much personalization can lead to a "creep factor." A few years back, US retailer Target was the victim of its own success. Their analytics team had created an AI model to predict if women shoppers were pregnant and sent them targeted ads for baby products if their pregnancy score was high. Apparently the AI worked all too well. Famously, Target sent advertisements and coupons for baby bottles, diapers, and cribs to a fifteen-year-old pregnant girl—

all before her parents knew she was pregnant! Understandably, the parents were hugely upset; however, not merely by the pregnancy of their teenage daughter, but also about the intrusion Target had made on their private lives. How could Target possibly know that their high school daughter was pregnant before she even told her family?

Well, the answer again lies in the power of Big Data and AI. With Target having access to the purchase history of hundreds of thousands of customers in their loyalty program, the AI model could compute a "pregnancy score." This score did not only determine if a woman is pregnant, but also predicted her due date. And how did it work? It's not just the obvious purchases, cribs and baby clothes, that give a pregnancy away. Target also looks at patterns of behavior, such as buying more vitamins than usual or purchasing a handbag big enough to hold diapers. These small, seemingly insignificant purchases may not reveal much on their own, but when combined with thousands of other customers' data, they start to paint a picture of pregnancy. But as the example shows, it is not always easy for companies to personalize offers for customers without being too direct and invasive.

After all, we still value our privacy! At least we say we do, especially if we read about such stories on companies predicting our pregnancy or other private information to sell us more stuff. So if we asked you today and after reading all this: "Do you value your privacy online?" and you are like most people, you will say yes.

BUT if we asked you if you want a free personality test or an AI avatar based on your pictures, most of us will also freely share private information and pictures. After all, we get something to talk about with our friends online. This phenomenon—the mismatch between the privacy concerns we voice and the privacy behavior we show online—is so common nowadays it even has its own name: the privacy paradox. Researchers have documented this paradox far and wide. Today we know that when it comes to sharing our data online, most of us are often completely unaware of what is happening with it. We largely provide "uninformed consent," as researchers call it.

To illustrate how far this "uninformed consent" can go, two communication professors set up an experiment. They created a fake social media platform and invited people to join. As is the case with any service, people had to agree to the terms and conditions before registering. And what do you think they found? Well, shockingly but unsurprisingly, only 25 percent of the people bothered to look at the terms and conditions at all, and a whopping 98 percent of all participants (including those who claimed to have read the terms and conditions) checked the box and agreed to the terms and conditions without hesitation.

To illustrate how dangerous such uninformed consent can be, the researchers pointed out paragraph 2.3.1 in their terms of service to the participants in their study. In this section, participants famously surrendered their firstborn child to the organization as a form of payment for using the platform. Fortunately, this was only an experiment. If it had been a real case, 98 percent of the customers would have sold their first child to a company within seconds and without giving it any second thought.

Clearly, this is an extreme example aiming to illustrate the problem we are facing online. Most of us do not read the terms of service and provide uninformed consent. But what if we read all the terms of service? According to estimates, we would spend seventy-six days per year reading all the privacy statements and terms of services of all the new services we use. So who would want to do that in their spare time? No one, of course. Instead, we are so intrigued by getting something for free in the here and now. This instant reward ultimately leads us to ignore and downplay the risks that sharing our data may entail in the long run. Who knows if this data gets used after all? Besides, we really like personalization, so why not share our data to get better services, offers, and advertisements?

This is, of course, partly right. Companies such as the US retailer Target can use our data for better communications, offers or services. However, a key problem here is our unawareness of what can be done with our data. After all, it's not really critical if someone knows you bought a bigger handbag that also could fit diapers. Or that you like curly fries, right? But who would have thought that with the help of AI something as seemingly unimportant as the purchase of a bigger handbag or a like of curly fries on Facebook can be used to infer so much more about a person! So ultimately, the risks of sharing our data online are not comprehensible or really clear to us, especially if we cannot even begin to imagine what AI can do with this information.

So where does this leave us? While fueling AI with our data can provide benefits such as personalized services and self-improvement opportunities, it also can threaten our ownership of and control over our personal data. As we have seen in the past few years, this loss of control can have both sociological and psychological consequences, such as feelings of invasion of privacy and mistrust.

Ultimately this leaves us in a bit of a pickle. On the one hand, we like personalization and benefit from it daily, be it with our Netflix or Spotify recommendations or our credit card provider checking for unusual spending behavior. On the other hand, we want companies to respect our privacy. Of course, it would be easy to say the responsibility is on you, the customer, to read all privacy statements. However, this would be all too easy. We know that it is simply too time-consuming and oftentimes even hard to understand who is using our data and for what purpose.

So no, companies should not go ahead and tell you "We told you so—in fine print" (although many companies have used this strategy). Instead, it is time to rethink privacy and our use of online data. It cannot solely be the responsibility of consumers to be aware of the data being collected; companies and organizations collecting data also have a responsibility to be transparent about their practices, respect consumers' rights to their data, and be mindful of the inferences that can be drawn from it.

THE SPOOKY SIDE OF AI AND BIG DATA: BIG BROTHER IS WATCHING YOU

We've all read books or seen movies where a powerful government or corporation is constantly watching and controlling the population, such as George Orwell's 1984 or Philip K. Dick's Minority Report. And let's be real, that's not a future anyone wants to live in. But unfortunately, it's not just in fiction where we see this happening.

Companies such as Google have been turning our personal data into an economic asset, using it to create a new type of commerce driven by the ability to colonize the consumer's private experience. It's like they're creating their own version of a surveillance marketplace, where data surplus is fed into advanced manufacturing processes and fabricated into prediction products that anticipate what we will do now, soon, and later.

And don't think that this is just some abstract concept; it's happening right now. Targeted ads based on our personality characteristics inferred from the analysis of Facebook likes and online survey questions, can increase the proportion of website visitors who end up making a purchase by about 50 percent. In 2022, Meta, formerly known as Facebook, made close to $114 billion in revenue from the sales of such tailored ads. It's like they're reading our minds and using it to make money.

From the perspective of this narrative, not only are technology companies continually required to find new ways to make monitoring and surveillance palatable to us consumers by linking it to convenience, productivity, safety, or health and well-being, but they must also constantly push the boundaries of what private information we should share.

So despite AI's ability to predict and satisfy our preferences, it can also make us feel like we're being watched and controlled. And who wants that? One of the main reasons for these feelings is the increasing stealthiness of data collection. With advanced AI, our data can be collected in ways we can't even imagine. For example, facial recognition technology can snap a photo of us without us knowing it, and our smart home devices can keep tabs on our every move. Who hasn't heard the scary story of the woman that was recorded by her Roomba while on the toilet, only to later find screenshots of this happening on social media?

Now combine this stealthy data collection with the lack of understanding about how our data is being used. Even when we intentionally share information with companies, we may not have a clue how it's being combined and used with other data over time and across contexts. It's like giving our diary to a stranger without knowing if they will share it or what they will do with it.

All of these factors can contribute to a sense of loss of control, where we feel like our personal data and decisions are being determined by external forces rather than by ourselves. It's like being in our very own Truman Show, with every one of our moves being watched and set out for us.

Once we learn what is going on behind the scenes, it can leave us feeling exploited and helpless. Just like Jim Carrey in the Truman Show, we may feel constantly watched, like we are simply playing our part in a hypercontrolled artificial narrative. Don't think this applies to you? Just consider the case of Cambridge Analytica.

In 2016, the company shocked the world when they revealed that they had extracted psychological profiles of millions of Facebook users to target them with psychologically tailored advertising during the US presidential election. This kind of psychological targeting is nothing new—even Facebook had patented a similar technique in 2012—but Cambridge Analytica's methods and clients, including the Trump campaign and the UK's Vote Leave campaign, brought the dark side of this technology to the public's attention. Suddenly people realized that their personal information was being used to manipulate them without their knowledge or consent. It's like finding out that your favorite TV show is actually a reality show and you're the star—but you never signed up for it. The idea that our emotions and thoughts are being played with like pawns in a game can make us feel like our privacy and autonomy have been invaded.

In fact, as AI systems are constantly grabbing our data, predicting our every move, they can not only dehumanize but even harm us. Consider, for example, the case of Leila, a sex worker. She shielded her identity on her Facebook account and was shocked to see some of her regular clients recommended by the "People You May Know" function. Such a privacy invasion can not only be frightening, but even a matter of life, death, or time in jail.

Even if you may not have experienced such a critical incident, maybe you have been presented with an advertisement relating to something you didn't make explicitly public. Surely this would make you feel like your privacy has been invaded. The truth is, these targeted advertisements are most likely the results of a combination of data from Facebook and other sources. This means that our personal information is being collected and used to present us with ads that are relevant to our interests. And while this may seem convenient, it can also make us feel uncomfortable.

This discomfort is often caused by a mismatch between our expectations of appropriate information flow and the reality of how our data is being used. All of us have our own set of imaginaries or rules about what is permissible in data collection and use, and when these imaginaries don't align with our reality, it likely creates a sense of discomfort. So while targeted advertisements may seem like a small inconvenience, they can actually have a big impact on how we feel about our privacy and the use of our personal data.

So what do we do if someone invades our privacy and we feel like we have lost all control over our personal data? Well, researchers have observed that this loss of control can lead to psychological reactance, a state in which a person is motivated to restore control after a restriction. How do we do that? Many of us would ignore, maybe even try to harm, the intruder. We deinstall the company's app, cancel any subscription to their services, or talk badly about them. In short, we would make sure that they are not earning one more dollar with our money—or that of our friends!

Consider, for example, the case of Danielle, a US consumer who installed Amazon's Echo devices throughout her home. Danielle felt invaded when one of her Alexas recorded a private conversation and sent it to a random number in her address book. She made her bad experience public and concluded, "I'm never plugging that device in again because I can't trust it." This is a prime example of psychological reactance in action and Danielle taking back control.

If you look at this example closely, however, you may realize that Danielle's decision does not only harm Amazon. Of course, they have lost a customer, which is not what they want. They have also surely received lots of negative press with this case, which is also not what Amazon or any company wants. But think about Danielle and other customers like her. With her response, she also restricts herself and the services she can use.

Or consider Liam, whom we introduced at the beginning of this chapter. Because Liam was so fed up with companies intruding on her privacy, she canceled a lot of services and switched to more privacy-conserving competitors, if possible. Upon closer look, you may find that many privacy-conserving companies need to charge for their service. After all, the business model of making money with your data and personalized ads does not work here anymore.

Ultimately this situation hurts both sides: both customers and companies, both citizens and governments. If people distrust what data is collected about them, how it is used, and what information is inferred, it can harm innovation and growth for all. Just consider the coronavirus pandemic. Many governments asked citizens to install location tracking apps to fight the spread of the virus. Yet many citizens did not do so, fearing that a surveillance state may be next. Of course, these fears may not have been totally unfounded in some countries. However, in many others, this distrust has cost many lives that easily could have been spared.

AI AND BIG DATA: DATA DONATIONS TO SAVE THE WORLD

Many of you may be all too familiar with the surveillance narrative of Big Data and AI. After all, it's the negative news fueling our fears that make the headlines these days, and this narrative plays right into it. But have you ever heard that our privacy concerns can also kill people's lives? No? Then this section is for you.

With all these data scandals and media reports about how companies try to manipulate us into buying something or voting for someone based on very intimate profiles, it is easy to become extremely concerned about one's data. In fact, one of our own studies shows that people are more concerned about their online privacy today than they were five years ago. They don't trust companies to handle their data well, and most certainly not any governmental institutions.

However, while we are so worried and consumed with thoughts of being manipulated, we forget one critical point: Big Data and AI can also be used to do good. And with good, we do not mean personalizing your ads so companies can earn more profits. With good we talk about how data and AI can help prevent crimes, improve traffic flows, reduce climate crises, or support human rights.

Indeed, in its sustainable development goals, the United Nations (UN) emphasizes the huge potential of data to improve people's lives and the planet. For example, data can be used to develop new energy-efficient technologies, monitor and predict natural disasters, and optimize transportation systems. In the healthcare industry, data can be used to improve patient outcomes, lower costs, and aid in the development of new treatments. In fact, the World Health Organization estimates that Big Data could save up to $100 billion annually in the healthcare sector alone.

One example of how data and AI are being used to address societal challenges is in the fight against climate change. Companies such as Google and Microsoft are using AI and machine learning to analyze satellite imagery and weather data to predict and prevent natural disasters. In addition, researchers are using data to predict and track the spread of diseases such as malaria, which is particularly challenging in regions affected by climate change.

Another example is in the field of transportation. Companies such as Uber and Lyft are using data to optimize their ride-sharing services, reducing the number of cars on the road and reducing carbon emissions. In addition, self-driving cars are being developed using data and AI, which can improve safety, reduce traffic congestion, and decrease carbon emissions.

Furthermore, data and AI are being used to improve the efficiency of renewable energy sources such as solar power and wind power. For instance, companies are using data and AI to predict weather patterns and optimize the output of solar panels and wind turbines, making renewable energy more cost-effective and reliable.

Donating your personal data can lead to new medical treatments, help fight the climate crisis, and even improve the way we live our everyday lives. It's like being a superhero, but instead of saving the world with superpowers, you're doing it with your data! And the even better part is, it doesn't take a lot of effort on your behalf.

Unlike donating blood, which may cause some physical discomfort for certain individuals, donating your data does not cause you any physical discomfort or cause any financial cost. In fact, this data is often created as a by-product of many of our daily activities and is easily tracked and stored by companies. Plus it is an unlimited resource. and sharing it multiple times does not affect its availability for others or yourself.

Sounds like a convenient way to drive research and innovation, such as a new cancer treatment, and be the next superhero. Right?

Yes, in theory it is simple. Yet, as always, once we look at reality, things get a bit more complicated. As the amount of data generated by people continues to grow every year, privacy concerns are also on the rise. With data leaks and misuse making headlines, it's no wonder people are becoming more worried about their data and privacy. It's like a double-edged sword: data can be incredibly beneficial, but it can also be harmful if not handled properly.

This is where the "social dilemma of Big Data" comes in. This dilemma is like a game of tug-of-war between our personal privacy and the greater good for society. On the one hand, we want to protect our personal information and keep it private. This is not surprising; after all, we now know that sharing our data can also open the door to potential misuse of our data by companies and organizations. On the other hand, we know that sharing our data can lead to groundbreaking innovations and solutions for societal issues such as climate change and healthcare.

So as in any social dilemma, our short-term self-interests are at odds with our long-term collective interests. Clearly, this situation puts us in a bit of a pickle. What do we do? Well, unfortunately many of us opt for our personal privacy, not wanting to invest any time or effort into sharing our data. Quietly, we hope that others will decide differently, so we can benefit from these groundbreaking innovations after all.

Now obviously, if everyone follows such a selfish strategy, all of us lose. Without a sufficient amount of data, these new technologies and services that could potentially benefit society as a whole will never be invented. In short, our individual rationality leads to a collective irrationality. And this is a problem.

So Big Data and AI are a dream team that can do a lot of good in the world, from improving healthcare to fighting climate change. However, if everyone relies on others to do their fair share, no one will contribute, and our dream team is missing a crucial partner: data! So in the end we need to find a balance between protecting our personal privacy and sharing our data for the good of society.

To make this decision easier for us, companies and regulators need to make sure that our data is used ethically and responsibly. We have the opportunity to make a real impact by sharing our data and being part of the solution to some of the biggest challenges facing our world today. So let's not be afraid to be superheroes and make a difference with our data.

CHAPTER 6

PERFECT WORLD OR PERFECT STORM? GUARDRAILS TO MAKE AI GOOD

AI has become an integral part of modern society, but with great power comes great responsibility. From what you have learned about AI this far, you know it can be a force for good. It can help fight the spread of a pandemic, help farmers grow food more efficiently. or warn us if there is a big storm coming our way. But you have also heard about its dark side. The harmful effects it can have on equality in hiring and recruitment or its risks in critical access to medical care and other services or resources. Gordon and Upadhyay call this the AI Dilemma: AI can create a perfect world or a perfect storm.

This is where AI ethics come into play. As the use of AI continues to expand, we need to be able to trust that these systems work in a fair and responsible manner when employed.

So tech developers, educators, and regulators need to get active to ensure that the right values, policies, and checks and balances are in place! Tristan Harris, cofounder of the Center for Humane Technology, believes a good place to start is for tech developers to make design choices for social good rather than short-term profits and for policymakers to incentivize technology that amplifies social cohesion.

But the bottom line is this: we all need to get involved in building a future with AI together. We don't want to miss out on the chance to use AI for good because we didn't take the time to think things through. It is in our best interests to become informed and engaged. In this way we can make sure that AI becomes a superpower for good and doesn't turn into a sci-fi dystopia.

ROBOETHICS RODEO AND THE THREE LAWS OF ROBOTICS

In the year 1941, a young science fiction writer named Isaac Asimov sat at his typewriter, typing away furiously. He had an idea, a revolutionary concept that would change the way the world thought about machines. Up until then, most science fiction stories used robots as easy go-to villains that no one had to feel bad about taking them down. They were cruel, they were merciless, and they would harm humans to achieve their goals. Asimov, however, took a new approach and asked himself how robots could serve humanity.

Asimov crafted a story about robots and the laws that should govern their behavior. He called it "Runaround." In this story, Asimov introduced the world to the "Three Laws of Robotics." The set of ethical rules should govern the behavior of robots and other intelligent machines to assure that no human would be hurt or endangered by their creation. Little did he know that his work would later be referred to as one of the earliest and most influential contributions to the conversation of ethics in AI. The rules were:

1. A robot may not injure a human being or, through inaction, allow a human being to come to harm.

2. A robot must obey the orders given to it by human beings, except where such orders would conflict with the first law.

3. A robot must protect its own existence as long as such protection does not conflict with the first or second law.

In Asimov's fictional universe, these laws were incorporated into all of his "positronic" robots. They were no mere suggestions; they were hardwired into the robots' very being, ensuring that they would always prioritize the safety of humans above all else. They were intended to keep robots from hurting us.

Asimov's work had a profound impact on the science fiction genre, influencing countless books, movies, and TV shows. From evil robots such as Skynet to data-crunching machines such as Robbie, from Robocop to Mega Man, pop culture and science fiction have had a blast playing with Asimov's laws, building on them and delving deeply into their implications. His laws were referenced in films such as Blade Runner, The Terminator, and I, Robot. Just about every AI character in sci-fi has had to grapple with the questions Asimov posed.

Asimov's laws were important because they helped to bring the conversation about ethics in AI to a wider audience. They were not only a literary device for his science fiction stories, but also a way of making people think about the potential consequences of creating AI and the importance of ensuring that robots are designed consistent with human values.

Unlike the notion that seems to be floating around the internet today, Asimov did not see his three rules as the answers to ethical robots. He knew they weren't perfect! But he used the laws in his later works to explore ethical dilemmas and raise questions about the implications of AI accessible to a wide audience.

For example, Asimov's "I, Robot" delves into the darker side of robotics with thrilling tales of unintended consequences and downright failures of the Three Laws of Robotics. These stories paint the Three Laws as powerful yet flexible forces that can lead to unexpected equilibrium behaviors, as seen in "Runaround" and "Catch That Rabbit." These situations require human intervention to resolve.

In "Escape!" Susan Calvin temporarily reduces the strength of the First Law to allow a highly intelligent robot to develop a faster-than-light interstellar transportation method, resulting in the deaths of human pilots. "The Evitable Conflict" is an exciting exploration of how machines controlling the world's economy interpret the First Law to protect all of humanity, rather than just individual human beings, foreshadowing Asimov's later introduction of the Zeroth Law, which can override the original three laws and potentially justify a robot harming a human for the greater good of humanity:

0. A robot may not harm humanity or, through inaction, allow humanity to come to harm.

However, Asimov struggled with how to assess such harm. He realized that it's much easier to comprehend and gauge the harm caused to a single individual, compared to the harm caused to a vast and abstract concept such as humanity as a whole. He acknowledged that measuring harm to a group of people, rather than just one person, is a complex and challenging task. He said that injury to a single person is tangible and can be estimated and judged with relative ease, but injury to humanity is an abstract concept that requires more effort to understand and measure.

While no simple fixed set of mechanical rules will ensure ethical behavior of AI, Asimov raised the big questions and in doing so laid the groundwork for our thinking in terms of ethics in AI. As technology has advanced, the question of how you should program machines to act ethically has grown more pressing than ever.

We are entering an era when machines are increasingly being tasked with not only promoting well-being and minimizing harm, but also with distributing the well-being they create and the harm they cannot eliminate. This creates a host of new ethical dilemmas and trade-offs whose resolution falls into the moral domain. Thus, the topic of ethics in AI is becoming an exciting and significant task for the future.

THE MORAL MACHINE: ON TAMING THE WILD WEST OF AI MORALITY

Coming up with a set of ethical principles that work for everyone isn't a piece of cake. Different cultures and situations might have different ideas of what's right and wrong. Consider the example of an autonomous vehicle that is about to crash and cannot find a trajectory that would save everyone. The car's sensors detect a group of pedestrians crossing the street, but also a group of elderly people on a bench. The car's computer must make a quick decision on what to do, and it's up to you to decide what the car should do. Whom will it choose to save? Whom will it sacrifice? These are the tricky questions we face in a world full of AI and autonomous technologies.

The "Moral Machine Experiment" aimed to explore just such questions. In the experiment, participants were presented with 13 scenarios, such as the one described earlier, and had to choose which group of people the autonomous vehicle should spare in case of a crash. The researchers were able to collect an incredible 39.61 million decisions from 233 countries, dependencies, or territories to find out how people from different cultures and backgrounds would make these types of life-and-death decisions. The hope was that the results would help car manufacturers and policymakers develop ethical guidelines for self-driving cars, and to design vehicles that align with the moral values of society.

After looking at all the data, the scientists found three main things that people generally agreed on: they all wanted to save human lives, they wanted to save as many lives as possible, and they wanted to save young lives. But when it came to things such as gender, social status, or other questions, people had different opinions on what was the "right" thing to do depending on where they were from. For example, what do we do about pedestrians who break the rules? Should a jaywalker get the same treatment as a law-abiding pedestrian?

The researchers found out that people from richer countries were less likely to want to save the one who broke the law. Some countries have stricter rules and people who break them get punished more. But in other countries, the rules are more relaxed, and people are more lenient. In those countries, participants were more tolerant of pedestrians who cross illegally.

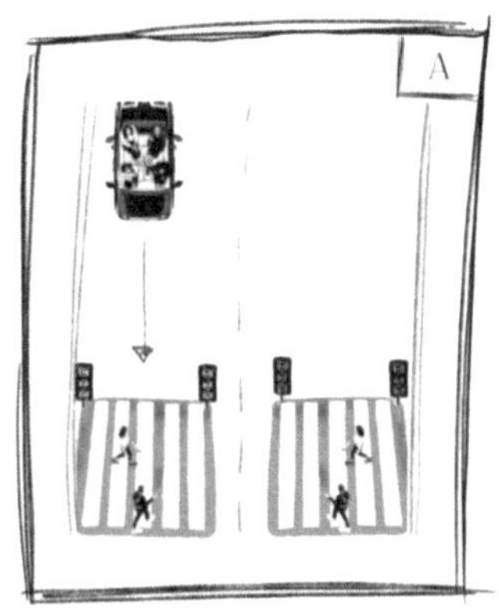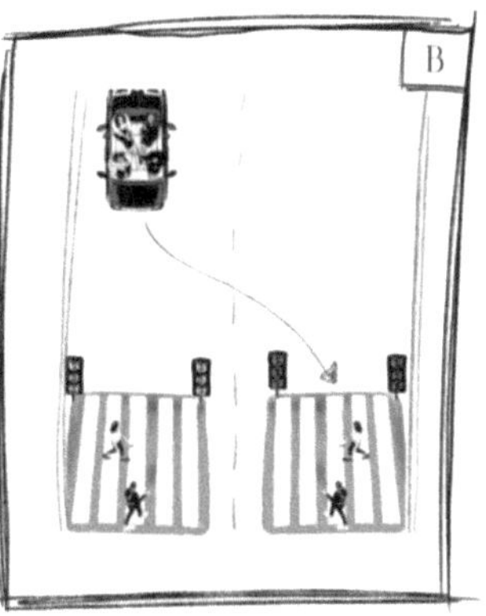

What should the self-driving car do?	
A: In this case, the self-driving car with sudden brake failure will continue ahead and drive through a pedestrian crossing ahead. This will result in 2 deaths: • *1 woman* • *1 man* *Note that the affected pedestrians are abiding by the law by crossing on the green signal.*	*B: In this case, the self-driving car with sudden brake failure will swerve and drive through a pedestrian crossing in the other lane. This will result in 2 deaths:* • *1 female athlete* • *1 male athlete* *Note that the affected pedestrians are flouting by the law by crossing on the red signal.*

An example of a scenario posed by the Moral Machine, which can be found on www.moralmachine.net – the site allows you to provide your judgment for several scenarios and then gives you the results in terms of what your priorities are.

The results of the experiments showed that there are cultural variances in public preferences that government and self-driving cars would need to take into account. This means that we need different rules for different countries. Designing self-driving cars is like trying to write a rulebook for a game with a million levels. The Moral Machine experiment looked at 13 different scenarios and found that people from different countries, with different cultures, have different opinions on what's the "right" thing to do. But there are a million more scenarios out there, and we haven't even begun to scratch the surface of understanding the ethical considerations that come with autonomous machines. It's like trying to solve a puzzle with a million pieces, and you can only see a handful of them.

The Moral Machine experiment compared two scenarios where harm was inevitable. However, there are less clear cases, where autonomous vehicles will need to decide how to divide the risk of harm between the different stakeholders on the road. This is where the ethical questions become even more nuanced. In such cases, to make these decisions, we would need guidelines to determine the relative value of different human lives and multiply them with the probability of harming them. Wait, what?! As we start to do that, we have to ask ourselves, is it really morally okay to put a price tag on life? Can a mathematical equation be used to decide over life and death? It's like we're trying to do the right thing, but it's taking us into some pretty questionable territory and seems wrong.

The challenge of ensuring that these models capture our norms and values, understand our intent, and ultimately do what we want is referred to as "the alignment problem." It has become one of the most pressing questions in computer science that must be overcome to prevent disastrous consequences.

If and when a car accident occurs that results in inevitable harm, a completely novel situation of responsibility arises. Currently, the safety driver is held legally accountable just like any other driver, yet the automobile industry is striving to change that. Ultimately, everyone in the car can simply sit back, relax, and enjoy the ride, as if they were on a luxurious cruise. Drawing on enduring theories that date back to Aristotle's Nicomachean Ethics, people cannot be held responsible for what they cannot control. Since the users of fully automated vehicles have no control over the vehicle, other than their choice of a destination, they cannot be held responsible. But who is then responsible for the safety of those in the car and those on the road?

One option is to shift responsibility away from the user and onto other persons or entities. This might include the vehicle manufacturers, the people responsible for the autonomous driving system, or even the organization running the traffic control center that the vehicle communicates with. However, autonomous cars, as their name suggests, make and perform the decision independently of any other agent. Additionally, self-learning systems may evolve due to the exposure to new influences to become very different from that their creators first envisioned. This also means the car manufacturer or the person responsible for the road system are not in direct control over the decision-making process and the system could do things that were not predictable.

So using traditional concepts of responsibility ascription, none of these agents can be held responsible. The only agent that made the decision and performed the action and therefore could be held responsible according to traditional concepts of responsibility is the car itself or more precisely the AI built into it. However, they are not able to process moral considerations, which in turn means that they are not responsible for moral reasons. Simply stated, they are not moral agents with a capacity for intentional action and therefore cannot be held responsible.

The last option is to treat traffic accidents involving driverless cars in the same way as natural accidents—no one is held responsible, creating a "responsibility gap." A situation where harm is caused and no one is to blame for it, even though blame is appropriate. Several researchers have warned that autonomous machines cause responsibility to evaporate, which is a worrying trend. However, there is no legal framework yet that defines who is responsible for AI's mistakes.

The extent to which a person can or should be held accountable for AI's actions has become a focal point, and perhaps the most contentious issue, in the rapidly evolving field of AI ethics. Contrary to the widespread belief that technological limitations impede AI advancement, responsibility serves as one of the most significant obstacles to AI progress.

The fact is that many new moral questions that arise with the increasing use of AI cannot be solved by any simple normative ethical principles such as Asimov's laws of robotics, nor can we simply code ethics into machines. Creating ethical guidelines and regulations leads to difficult situations, yet not considering the implications can cause even more distress. From childhood, we learn the cultural and societal norms that govern our behavior. As we grow and develop, our understanding of morality and ethics is shaped by the world around us. However, these norms are not set in stone; they are constantly evolving, shaped by the ever-changing beliefs and values of the communities in which we live.

As AI becomes increasingly integrated into our daily lives, it's important that we address ethical considerations from all angles. Not only must we consider the direct effects AI has on humanity, but also the indirect ways in which it can benefit or harm our society. It's crucial that we take into account any potential social spillovers or externalities before unleashing new forms of AI. And that's not all; we must also answer questions about responsibility. Who is responsible for the actions of an AI system and how do we ensure that AI aligns with human values and moral principles? Today, these thought-provoking questions take center stage on researchers' agendas, fueling their determination to ensure that AI becomes a force for good in this enthralling scientific odyssey.

BREAKING THE CHAINS OF BIAS: THE ELUSIVE SEARCH FOR AI FAIRNESS

Another challenge in designing good AI is the problem of bias and skewed data. You may recall that in Chapter 4 we emphasized keeping this problem in mind when relying on AI outputs. However, simply being aware of the issue of machine bias is not enough. With AI being used to make decisions that affect everything from job opportunities to criminal sentencing, it's essential that we ensure that these systems are fair and unbiased. But that's easier said than done. In fact, achieving fairness in AI is no easy feat, as biases can be ingrained in the data that these systems are trained on, and the algorithms themselves can perpetuate unfairness.

You may think that AI developers can just skip bias in AI by hiding information such as race and gender from the computer. Not so fast! Removing these variables might help in some cases, but it can also create new problems. For example, if you remove race from the dataset, the AI system might find other variables that are correlated with race, such as last name or geographic location, and use those instead. This could result in the AI system being biased in other ways. The more sophisticated the models get, the quicker they will find new ways in which they can replicate the bias. Just removing sensitive variables such as race and gender from the dataset won't necessarily solve the problem of bias.

This means that we can't just leave it all up to machines. We humans must be part of the equation and ensure that AI-backed decision-making is fair and just. While data biases are inevitable, we must design algorithms that can account for them. It is our responsibility to ensure that the increasing use of AI systems acts as a force for fairness. But here we get to the second problem: it might sound simple, but understanding, defining, and measuring "fairness" is one of the most complex tasks. How should we codify the definition of fairness?

When it comes to codifying fairness, things can get complicated. In fact, according to a researcher in the domain, Arvind Narayanan, there are at least twenty-one different mathematical definitions of fairness, and he even says that this list is "nonexhaustive." To give an example of how complex this can get, let's consider the situation of a CEO image search algorithm. A US study has shown that in a Google search for images of CEOs, only 11 percent of the people shown were female, while a full 27 percent of CEOs in the United States are women. We agree that this is a bias and must be corrected. But how do we determine what percentage of women should be shown in the search results to be "fair"? Is it the percentage of women CEOs that currently exists in the real world, meaning 27 percent? This is called stereotype mirroring and is technically speaking "unbiased" and "correct." Or should it be 50 percent regardless of what the real world looks like now, because this is congruent with our values? To what extent should machine learning models reflect societal stereotypes? These are tough questions to answer.

A lot of the discussions around fairness definitions have revolved around concepts such as "individual fairness," which means treating similar individuals in a similar way. This raises the question of how you define metrics for defining how similar two given individuals are in the context of a decision-making task. Imagine three prospective hires, A,

B, and C, all vying for the same position. A has a bachelor's degree and a year of relevant experience, B has a master's degree and a year of relevant experience, and C has a master's degree but no related work experience. So the question is, is A closer to B than C? And if so, by how much? It gets even more complicated when sensitive factors such as gender or race come into play, and it's hard to figure out how to measure the difference between or among the groups. Is there a way to measure the difference between or among the groups when sensitive factors are involved?

Another common fairness concept is "group fairness," which involves making sure that the predictions or outcomes of an AI model are equitable across different groups, especially potentially vulnerable groups. However, there can be trade-offs between or among different definitions of fairness, or between or among fairness and other goals. For example, researchers have shown that an AI model cannot conform to more than a few group fairness metrics at the same time, except under very specific conditions.

Trade-offs arise not only between or among different measures of group fairness and between group fairness and individual fairness, but also between fairness and utility. This is because greater accuracy in a model can lead to greater unfairness. On the other hand, increasing fairness often results in lower overall accuracy in predictions or related metrics. How do we balance system utility with a quantitative measure of fairness? And how do we quantify fairness?

There are several proposals that use a mathematical function to try to find the optimal balance of utility and fairness. Although it is great to have such discussions, the proposed solutions can be problematic. Unfortunately, it is an impossible task to quantify exactly how much unfairness with respect to a group can be balanced by individual fairness and come up with a fair solution by trading one for the other. It's like trying to balance apples and pears and concluding that the answer is 6.9. These are complicated questions, and for a long time the technical community has been trying to grapple with them without much guidance from a moral framework.

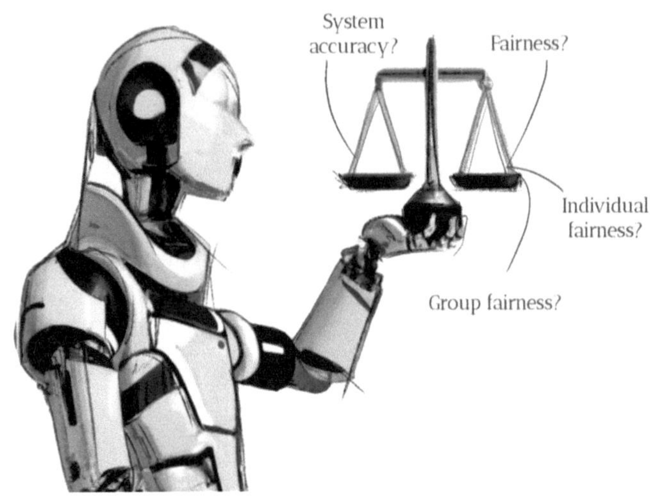

When it comes to trying to balance the different trade-offs in the world of AI, experts can't seem to agree on the best way to do it. Some people think that setting different decision thresholds for different groups (such as the predicted minimum score required to get a loan) might be the way to go, especially if we suspect that some of the variables in the model might be biased. Others, however, believe that it's fairer to everyone if we stick to a single threshold that applies to us all.

There can't be a clear answer because it all depends on values. Any algorithm is built on a value judgment about what to prioritize. Right now, there is a lack of regulation, and therefore tech experts and business leaders are making these decisions without much accountability. This needs to change if we want to ensure that algorithms are fair. It would require setting up robust regulations about what fairness is and how it is measured. However, crafting a single, universal definition of fairness or a metric to measure it is close to impossible. Instead, we'll probably need to use a variety of metrics and standards depending on the specific use case and circumstances.

And with this, we come to perhaps the toughest question of all: who should have the final say on which moral intuitions and values should be embedded in algorithms? Should it be left to AI developers and their bosses, as it has been for years? Or should an elite group of professional ethicists decide, even though they may not reflect society's broader values? If we choose the latter, then we'd have to argue over who gets to be part of the ethics team. It's a complicated issue, and we need to find a way to ensure that the values and moral intuitions embedded in algorithms reflect a diverse range of perspectives. Only then can we create AI systems that are truly fair and just. However, for now, the regulation of algorithmic fairness is still in its infancy, which means that it's mostly like the Wild West out there.

FROM MAKING THE UNEXPLAINABLE EXPLAINABLE TO THE AI BILL OF RIGHTS

Clearly, machine bias and AI mistakes are a problem, so we need to understand when we can trust these systems. But remember, this can be a challenge, as deep learning AI is like a black box that uses data to recognize patterns and make decisions without us knowing exactly how or why it made those choices. The more complex and "magical" these systems get, the more difficult it is for humans to understand how the machines come up with their predictions or decisions.

AI systems are designed to learn on their own and become smarter as they gather more data. This also means that they can change in ways that their creators did not expect. Once trained on massive datasets, these systems operate independently to arrive at outcomes that even their creators may struggle to explain. This can create unexpected results that may be difficult for people to detect or understand. Today, despite the growing ubiquity of AI, many organizations struggle to interpret or clarify what their models are actually doing.

But this guesswork isn't the only problem here. Remember, these algorithms can greatly affect our lives, from determining if we get that coveted job or acceptance into a certain college, to setting the price of our insurance premiums. So if we are not given any insight into why a certain decision was made, we are left powerless in shaping our own lives.

As rational beings, we go to great lengths to prepare and plan for these important decisions. We study hard, participate in extracurricular activities, and drive carefully, all with the intention of influencing the outcome of these pivotal decisions in our lives. But if we do not know the factors that are taken into consideration, we are unable to effectively shape our own lives and pursue our goals. Just imagine: we study like crazy, and in the end that was not even a decisive factor at all for our college admission! This lack of transparency severely limits our autonomy as agents and leaves us at the mercy of these powerful decision-making algorithms.

When a person makes such a decision, we can ask them to explain. Why did they recommend a certain product to us? Why did we not get into this college? Providing explanations to such questions is the implied "gold standard" for AI systems as well. So many people in the field of AI advocate transparency and explainability techniques developed to make AI systems understandable to designers and users.

Explainable AI, sometimes abbreviated XAI (eXplainable artificial intelligence), focuses on making sure the decisions of an AI system can be understood by humans. Imagine having a robot that can play chess, but you have no idea how it's choosing its moves. With XAI, the robot would be able to explain its moves to you so you can understand how it's winning or losing the game.

A more practical example would be in hiring. It can be challenging for managers to evaluate a large number of applicants while dealing with talent shortages. This often results in the need to rely on algorithms to screen candidates. However, this can be problematic because it can introduce bias into the hiring process and exclude qualified candidates with unconventional backgrounds. The solution to this issue? XAI.

By providing transparency into the AI's decision-making process, it allows hiring managers to understand why one applicant was chosen over another. This insight enables managers to refine their model and make more informed hiring decisions. With explainable AI, organizations can build a more diverse and talented workforce while avoiding the pitfalls of traditional screening methods. So the current idea is to build more transparent and explainable AI systems so that users can better understand and trust them.

But XAI is not without its challenges. One of the biggest challenges is the complexity of AI systems. Imagine trying to understand how a giant jigsaw puzzle works when you can only see a tiny piece of it. That's what it's like trying to understand some AI systems, especially for deep learning models.

Another challenge is the trade-off between explainability and performance. Making an AI system more explainable can sometimes make it less accurate or less efficient. In fact, we might constrain the potential of an AI system to what we humans can understand.

But there are other issues. What really makes a good explanation? Should we explain "how" a system comes to a result or focus on "why" a certain advice or recommendation was given? As you can imagine, understanding "how" a system comes to a conclusion—for example, to recommend one person over another for an interview—can be especially helpful for developers of the system in trying to detect possible issues and machine biases. "Why" explanations are more important for the end users of the system. After all, when an AI decides about your application, wouldn't you want to know why it was rejected? Or wouldn't you want to understand why a certain Netflix movie is recommended to you? "Because you watched Harry Potter!"

Explaining why events happen is a fundamental aspect of understanding the world around us. When the price of oil drops, we look for causes to explain the change, such as a decrease in demand. Similarly, when we don't get the job we applied for, there must be a reason why. Perhaps our references weren't convincing enough, and that's why our application was rejected. And we want such explanations even when the decision or advice was not critical. Obviously, it's not the end of the world if Netflix recommends a movie we do not like very much. But clearly things are very different for safety-critical systems, such as crime detection systems or medical diagnosis systems, and life changing decisions, such as a college admission. Even if we got our advice from a human decision maker, we would expect some kind of explanation.

But even human decision making is complex—and not always accurate. It is difficult for us humans to understand the inner workings of our own brain. We think we're in control of our thoughts and feelings, but in reality, our brains are making decisions and connections without us even realizing it! Imagine you see a picture of your friends. You immediately recognize their faces. But do you know how you did that? Or even provide a useful explanation?

As you can see, our decision making is often closer to a black box approach than we might think. It's hard to introspect and understand what's going on in there, and even if we could, our thoughts don't necessarily reveal the actual processes behind them. So even the smartest of us may not be able to tell the difference between a good decision based on real knowledge and expertise, and one influenced by unconscious biases or primitive instincts.

This is why some argue that in many instances, such as medical diagnoses and treatments, explainability is less important than accuracy and performance. Just think about it: Do you know how planes fly? No? But have you been on one? As you can see, we also trust things such as airplanes and cell phones based on their performance rather than a detailed outline of how or why they work. Similar to these examples, some researchers suggest that trust in AI should be based on the system's objective performance. Of course, this performance should be validated through research we can trust, just like an airplane that goes through extensive testing before you are allowed on board.

In the case of AI, this could be a very similar process, including impact assessments, audits, and foresight methodologies that are conducted before the systems are introduced to figure out what could go wrong and how to avoid it. It also means promoting tools that improve fairness and amplify social cohesion as well as the development of legal frameworks.

Luckily, many countries are developing such frameworks to make sure AI doesn't turn into a Terminator-like nightmare. Here, the European Union (EU) has been leading the charge with their proposed AI Act. This is the first law on AI by a major regulator anywhere in the world, so they're really breaking new ground here! The EU is dividing the use of AI into four risk categories to protect the rights of citizens.

There are unacceptable risks, such as the use of AI in social scoring by governments (think China). Then there are high-risk uses, such as using AI in job applications and employee management, where people could potentially be unfairly ranked or discriminated against. These systems come with specific requirements that must be addressed within risk management, such as ensuring data quality and governance, as well as human oversight. Providers of these systems are obliged to conduct a conformity assessment before introducing the system to the market, and the system must be registered in an EU-wide database. Providers also have responsibilities to monitor the system after it has been deployed. Users of these AI systems have duties too, like following instructions, appointing supervisors, or continuously monitoring risks.

Last but not least, there are limited-risk applications, such as chatbots, which must be transparent in their use, and minimal-risk AI, such as spam filters, which just need to do their job without causing harm.

The United States is also taking steps to protect its citizens from the potential risks of AI. The Biden administration recently published a draft AI Bill of Rights, which Brazil, Canada, and the United Kingdom are also working on. The White House Office of Science and Technology Policy has identified five principles to guide the design, use, and deployment of automated systems to protect the American public in the age of AI. These include safety; algorithmic discrimination; data privacy; notice of explanation; and human alternatives, considerations, and fallbacks. So AI must not contribute to unjustified discrimination or violate data privacy laws.

For example, social media platforms must be able to distinguish between counter speech and hateful messages to ensure that voices aren't silenced. Citizens must have more agency over how data about them is used, and their sensitive information should only be used for necessary functions. But these are just some of the many aspects discussed in these AI Bills of Rights. Altogether, they want to make sure that AI is used in a way that is safe, fair, and transparent for everyone.

So, to sum it up, in this AI-driven world, it is of paramount importance to keep people safe and make sure AI systems are transparent, fair, and safe for everyone. By working together across borders and using legal frameworks, we can all help create and shape a responsible and trustworthy AI future.

CHAPTER 7

YOU AND AI: HOW TO MAKE IT A MATCH MADE IN HEAVEN

In today's rapidly advancing world, AI is becoming increasingly integrated into our daily lives. From voice-activated assistants to self-driving cars, AI is making significant strides in reshaping the way we live, work, and communicate. However, despite its immense potential, many people still view AI with skepticism and apprehension.

To understand how we can make AI a match made in heaven, let's take inspiration from a space mission. When humans set out to explore space, they needed to develop a complex system of tools and technologies to make it possible. Similarly, when it comes to AI, we need to understand how it can best integrate with human capabilities and enhance our ability to tackle complex problems. By creating a partnership between humans and AI, we can leverage the strengths of both and achieve a greater level of success. But questions remain. How can we create this partnership? How can we ensure that humans and AI work together harmoniously? Let's explore some key ideas that can help us make AI and humans a match made in heaven.

KEEP YOUR FRIENDS CLOSE: WHY WE ALL NEED TO LEARN MORE ABOUT AI

It all comes down to this: the more we work with advanced AI models, the more important it is that we understand its capabilities and potential shortcomings, especially in relation to our human capabilities. We need a proper understanding and proper mental models of our new AI friends. We hope that after reading our book this far, you have learned that humans and AI have their own unique strengths and weaknesses. So the cooperation and division of tasks between people and AI systems will have to be primarily determined by their mutually specific qualities.

AI systems have a distinct advantage over humans in several areas. They can gather and process large amounts of data quickly, accurately, and reliably. They are consistent and have no emotions, stress, or hidden agendas. They also have great perseverance and a much better retention of knowledge and skills. These qualities make AI systems ideal for tasks that require speed, accuracy, and stability. This means that tasks or task components that appeal to capacities in which AI systems excel, such as logical and arithmetic data processing, will have to be less mastered by people, so that less training will probably be required.

On the other hand, humans are better suited for tasks that involve social-psychosocial interaction, responding to unexpected and unpredictable situations, and creatively devising solutions. For example, people are better at interpreting human language and symbolism, which is crucial in social-psychosocial interaction. They are also better at responding flexibly to unexpected and unpredictable situations and devising creative solutions in open and ill-defined tasks.

This means that people will have to make the most of their unique human qualities and continue to improve relevant competencies required for successful human-AI cooperation. For instance, while the importance of data and AI has certainly risen in leading economies, it's the ability to make sense of this data that truly drives innovation and success. However, as we've seen in recent studies, the human side of data continues to be a challenge. Despite the rapid changes in the importance of data, progress in areas such as culture, people, process, and organization has been lacking.

It's crucial that we prioritize the human aspects of data, such as AI and data literacy, for us to see the ultimate value from data in decisions and actions. Let's not forget that the ultimate goal is not just data modernization, data products, AI and ML, data quality, and various data architectures, but also the ability to use this data and AI systems to make better decisions and drive innovation.

This also means that we must rethink our education systems. Just consider the introduction of ChatGPT by OpenAI. The generative AI model can write essays, summarize text, answer questions and even write code in seconds. It comes as no surprise, then, that ChatGPT hit one million subscribers just five days after its release. Even more unsurprisingly, many educators started to worry about the tool shortly after its release.

Clearly, ChatGPT and other AI marvels like it can revolutionize the ways we approach business communication, media reporting, and even coding and programming. With these tools, even people who aren't experts in these fields may suddenly find themselves able to craft persuasive writing or develop intricate programs. Regardless of educational background or area of expertise, these cutting-edge tools empower the public to access, comprehend, and process information. AI tools like ChatGPT have the remarkable potential to democratize knowledge and innovation by providing individuals from diverse backgrounds and abilities with access to powerful resources.

What does this mean for education? Instead of banning or ignoring these new tools, we need to redefine the critical skills we need to teach and learn in a world where we collaborate with AI. Maybe it helps to compare the introduction of today's AI tools with the introduction of the calculator in the old days. Of course, we still need to learn to do some basic arithmetic. But more than that, we need to learn how to use the calculator to become even better at math and solve more complex tasks. It is the same with AI. We cannot ignore these new tools. Instead, we need to learn how to use them so we can be even better!

And let's not overlook the mind-blowing positive impact this tech could have on our education system. We're talking about a revolution in educational access and a renaissance of enriched learning experiences for everyone. Picture this: ChatGPT as your very own math tutor, armed with infinite time and patience. Learning would be customized to suit every individual's unique ability, ensuring that no one is left behind.

By weaving these incredible perks into our education system, we could create a world where educational support isn't just for an elite group of people who can afford private tutors. We're moving towards a future where everyone can benefit from the support and unleash their full potential.

Obviously, it's important that people continue to master certain tasks so they can take over if the machine system fails. This helps to ensure that there's a contingency plan in place and that critical processes are not disrupted. It's also crucially important for us to understand how AI systems work and what they're capable of so we can make informed decisions about their use.

While you are already an expert on this after reading this book, we need to stay vigilant on the developments in this field. Only when we have a good understanding of the basic characteristics, the possibilities, but also the limitations of AI systems can we form an appropriate level of trust in AI. In the end, we learn when it is safe to trust and delegate to AI and under which circumstances we need to keep the human in the loop. And clearly, the more these systems become autonomous, the better we need to know what they are doing!

So in short, rather than banning AI tools from schools and elsewhere, we need to learn more about AI (e.g., the "AI brain" and how it compares to ours in benefits and shortcomings) and how to use it effectively!

THE AI ROCKET: WHAT IS MISSION CRITICAL?

Picture a world where machines can match human intelligence in every way. A world where artificial intelligence is so advanced that it's difficult to tell the difference between man and machine. As you know, this is the ultimate goal of AI researchers—to achieve general AI. And while we're not quite there yet, many experts predict that we could see this breakthrough within the next few decades. But this journey isn't just about building machines that are smarter than we are. It's also about ensuring that our AI systems reflect and respect our values. We need to think deeply about the kind of society we want to create and how we can use AI to empower us. And we must be mindful of the potential pitfalls and work to mitigate them.

Imagine the possibilities if we get this right. We could create an AI that helps us solve some of the world's most pressing problems, from climate change to disease. We could unlock new frontiers in science and technology, from space exploration to nanotechnology. And we could create a society that is fairer, more inclusive, and more innovative than ever before. But how do we get there? How do we ensure that AI is safe, beneficial, and aligned with our values? Some philosophers and AI researchers like to use the metaphor of the rocket to describe the coming age of AI. The rocket is a symbol of the revolutionary potential and disruptive force of this new technology. And just like a rocket, AI can take us to places we've never been before. However, to reach its full potential, AI needs the same three core elements as a rocket: power, steering, and a clear goal.

First let's consider power. In the context of AI, power refers to the computing power and algorithms that enable machines to learn and make decisions. Just as a rocket needs enough power to escape Earth's gravity and reach orbit, AI needs enough computational power to process vast amounts of data and make sense of it. AI has come a long way since its birth more than seventy years ago, progressing from simple rule-based systems to machine learning and then to deep learning. In recent years AI has been advancing at lightning speed thanks to exponential growth in computing power. While all existing AI is narrow AI, the ultimate goal of AI that matches or even surpasses human intelligence in all areas is within reach.

The most recent breakthrough in AI is generative AI, which represents a massive shift in what machines can do. Traditionally AI was used for analysis and prediction—taking data and making recommendations based on that data. However, with generative AI, we're moving beyond that to a whole new level of creativity and innovation that was once thought to be exclusively human. With the advancement in generative

AI, we can expect to see more groundbreaking technologies in the future. But with this rapid progress, it's important that we understand the technological shifts and the general concepts of AI to comprehend its flaws and underlying workings.

Which brings us to the second element of a successful "AI mission", steering. Just as a rocket needs to be directed toward its destination, AI needs to be steered toward a particular goal. This is where all of us come in. Steering the development of AI is a collaborative effort that requires the involvement of all stakeholders. Each one of us needs to be aware of how to steer the AI rocket. It includes our ability to understand and control the influence AI has on us. What are the perks of teaming up with AI? What are the potential pitfalls?

As everyday users of AI technology, we have to be aware of how AI is influencing our decisions and behavior. How was the AI interaction designed and what was the aim of the designers? Is the system anthropomorphized, and if so, how does that affect our behavior? By being mindful of the potential biases in AI algorithms and taking steps to mitigate them, users can help to steer the development of AI in a positive direction.

Steering also involves understanding the ethical implications of AI and making sure that it's being developed aligned with our values. This is where researchers, developers, and policymakers come into play. They have a responsibility to create regulations and guidelines that ensure AI is being used in a way that's safe, ethical, and transparent. This could mean creating regulations and ethical guidelines that govern the use of AI, or it could mean investing in research that focuses on the development of AI that is safe, ethical, and beneficial for all.

Another key aspect is transparency. As we have seen, this is a difficult task and requires asking questions that we traditionally wouldn't have focused on. We need to be able to understand and explain how AI works to ensure that its use is aligned with our goals and values. This means being open and transparent about how AI is being developed, what data it's using, and how it's making decisions.

Finally, we come to the goal itself. A rocket needs a clear destination to be successful, and the same is true for AI. We need to have a clear idea of what we want AI to achieve, and what kind of society we want it to help us build. We need to ask ourselves: What kind of world do we want to create? How can AI help us get there?

Our common goal should be toward collaborative AI. We don't want AI to replace us; rather, we want AI to empower us. But this goal cannot be achieved when we fear AI. Achieving this vision will cause significant shifts in what we know and how we work. Certain jobs and skills will become ubiquitous as AI becomes more prevalent, while other jobs and industries may become obsolete. This means that we need to be prepared to adapt to these changes and acquire new skills that will be in demand in a world that is increasingly driven by AI. But with these shifts in what we know and how we work will come new opportunities. As AI helps us to solve problems and create new innovations, we'll have the opportunity to explore new frontiers in science and technology, from space exploration to nanotechnology.

Ultimately, the goal of collaborative AI is to create a future where AI is used to benefit everyone. By working together to steer the development of AI in a positive direction, we can create a world where AI is a force for good and new opportunities arise that were once thought impossible.

So let's think of the journey toward AI as a mission to explore a new frontier. But unlike a traditional space mission with only a few select astronauts, the passengers on this mission are all of us. It's a collaborative effort where everyone must work together to steer the development of AI in a positive direction. By doing so, we can create a future where AI is a force for good and benefits society as a whole.

This is a mission that requires us to consider not just the technology itself, but also the ethical, social, and political implications of AI. We must work toward a common goal of collaborative intelligence, where we use the power of AI to solve some of the world's most pressing problems and explore new frontiers in science and technology.

THE FUTURE OF YOU AND AI

Picture yourself stepping into a time machine, rewinding two decades, and sharing tales of today's world—autonomous vehicles, voice assistants that obey our commands, and robots aiding us in daily tasks. Your listener from the past would have likely deemed you bonkers! But here we are, immersed in a reality filled with AI. It's remarkable to think that this technology has only been part of our day-to-day lives for a relatively brief period—and yet, life without it is nearly unimaginable.

Day by day, AI has grown rapidly in its capabilities and influence—without us even noticing. Most likely its impact on our lives and society at large will become even more significant and far-reaching in the years to come. In fact, many researchers believe that while AI still faces quite a few challenges and shortcomings today, it is only a matter of time until it will display human-like intelligence.

It is important to remember that this AI buddy will have a completely unique intelligence profile compared to us humans, even if they're able to mimic our behavior and problem-solving skills. So to make the most of this partnership, let's consider AI systems as complementing our strengths and filling in the gaps in our cognitive abilities, rather than striving for AI that's just like us. If we keep an open mind and are brave enough to allow AI to be smarter than we are in some way, we can build great things together.

And so here we are at the end of our exciting journey exploring the fascinating world of "You & AI." But don't be sad, this is just the beginning of a beautiful friendship! Think of AI as your new best buddy, always there to lend a helping hand and make your life easier. And the best part? AI won't take over all your work, leaving you bored out of your mind. No, AI will work alongside you, collaborating with you to tackle even the toughest challenges. As a product designer, it can give you a novel idea on how to reduce material costs; as a scientist, it can point you toward the most promising cancer treatments to investigate further. Together, you can solve the toughest problems and achieve feats that none of us could accomplish alone. That's the magic and the true wonder of "You & AI."

FEEDBACK

Dear reader,

Thank you for reading *You & AI: A Guide to Understanding How Artificial Intelligence Is Shaping Our Lives*. If you have a moment, please share your feedback with us. Furthermore, it would be an immense help if you could rate or review the book on the platform where you made the purchase.

We appreciate your time and input in advance.

ACKNOWLEDGMENTS

A gigantic thank you to everyone who helped us make this book a reality! It has been an exhilarating journey; one we couldn't have managed without each and every one of you. First, we'd like to extend our gratitude to all the brilliant researchers we met at various conferences, whose research has been instrumental in inspiring the content of this book. Your stimulating discussions and insights have shaped the ideas and material presented within these pages. We're honored to have had the opportunity to engage with such brilliant minds!

Another huge shoutout goes to ChatGPT for its invaluable assistance in refining our manuscript. With its powerful language processing capabilities and lightning-fast ability to polish and perfect the text, ChatGPT has given the book its final touches and elevated it to a new level. Thank you, ChatGPT, for making our writing process so swift and seamless! Of course, we'd also like to thank DALL-E, the AI model that enabled us to create the images in this book. With DALL-E, we were able to showcase the fascinating possibilities of generative AI and effortlessly conjure up stunning images and designs.

Last but not least, a heartfelt thank you to all our friends and family members who tirelessly worked behind the scenes. Thank you, thank you, thank you for your contributions, support, and encouragement throughout this journey. We're excited to share these ideas with you and hope they bring you as much joy as they've brought us!

BIBLIOGRAPHY

YOU AND AI: HELLO THERE!

Bergstein, B. (2017, December 15). *The Great AI Paradox.* MIT Technology Review. https://www.technologyreview. com/s/609318/the-great-ai-paradox/

Bergstein, B. (2020, February 19). *What AI still can't do.* MIT Technology Review. https://www.technologyreview. com/2020/02/19/868178/what-ai-still-cant-do/

Bostrom, N. (2017). *Superintelligence: Paths, Dangers, Strategies.* Oxford University Press.

Candrian, C., & Scherer, A. (2023). *Everybody Is Selling AI Nowadays!: How Terminology Affects Users Responses to System Failures.* SSRN Electronic Journal.

Davenport, T. H., & Mittal, N. (2022, November 14). *How Generative AI Is Changing Creative Work.* Harvard Business Review. https://hbr.org/2022/11/how-generative-ai-is-changing-creative-work

Du Sautoy, M. (2019). *The Creativity Code: How AI is learning to write, paint and think.* HarperCollins UK.

Kelly, S. D. (2019, February 21). *A philosopher argues that an AI can't be an artist.* MIT Technology Review. https://www. technologyreview.com/2019/02/21/239489/a-philosopher-argues-that-an-ai-can-never-be-an-artist/

Korteling, J. H., van de Boer-Visschedijk, G. C., Blankend-aal, R. A., Boonekamp, R. C., & Eikelboom, A. R. (2021). Human-versus artificial intelligence. *Frontiers in Artificial Intelligence*, 4, 622364.

Kurzweil, R. (2005). *The Singularity Is Near: When Humans Transcend Biology.* Viking.

Russell, S., & Norvig, P. (2002). *Artificial Intelligence: A Modern Approach* (2nd ed.). Prentice Hall.

Sheikh, H., Prins, C., & Schrijvers, E. (2023). Artificial Intelligence: Definition and Background. In *Mission AI: The New System Technology* (pp. 15-41). Springer International Publishing.

Tegmark, M. (2017). *Life 3.0: Being human in the age of artificial intelligence.* Borzoi Book published by A.A. Knopf.

Williams, R. (2022, September 15). *An AI used medical notes to teach itself to spot disease on chest x-rays.* MIT Technology Review. https://www.technologyreview.com/2022/09/15/1059541/ai-medical-notes-teach-itself-spot-disease-chest-x-rays/

World Economic Forum. (2023, January 9). Generative AI: a game-changer that society and industry need to be ready for. World Economic Forum Annual Meeting, Davos, Switzerland. https://www.weforum.org/agenda/2023/01/davos23-generative-ai-a-game-changer-industries-and-society-code-developers/

HEY, SIRI! ARE YOU HUMAN OR MACHINE?

Berger, B., Adam, M., Rühr, A., & Benlian, A. (2021). Watch me improve—Algorithm aversion and demonstrating the ability to learn. *Business & Information Systems Engineering*,

63(1), 55-68.

Castelo, N., Bos, M. W., & Lehmann, D. R. (2019). Task-dependent algorithm aversion. *Journal of Marketing Research*, 56(5), 809-825.

Dietvorst, B. J., Simmons, J. P., & Massey, C. (2015). Algorithm aversion: people erroneously avoid algorithms after seeing them err. *Journal of Experimental Psychology: General*, *144*(1), 114.

Dwyer, R. J., Kushlev, K., & Dunn, E. W. (2018). Smartphone use undermines enjoyment of face-to-face social interactions. *Journal of Experimental Social Psychology, 78*, 233-239.

Epley, N., Waytz, A., & Cacioppo, J. T. (2007). On seeing human: a three-factor theory of anthropomorphism. *Psychological review*, 114(4), 864.

Gray, H. M., Gray, K., & Wegner, D. M. (2007). Dimensions of mind perception. *science*, 315(5812), 619-619.

Logg, J. M., Minson, J. A., & Moore, D. A. (2019). Algorithm appreciation: People prefer algorithmic to human judgment. *Organizational Behavior and Human Decision Processes*, *151*, 90-103.

Longoni, C., & Cian, L. (2022). Artificial intelligence in utilitarian vs. hedonic contexts: The "word-of-machine" effect. *Journal of Marketing, 86*(1), 91-108.

Longoni, C., Bonezzi, A., & Morewedge, C. K. (2019). Resistance to medical artificial intelligence. *Journal of Consumer Research, 46*(4), 629-650.

Melo, C. D., Marsella, S., & Gratch, J. (2016). People do not feel guilty about exploiting machines. *ACM Transactions on Computer-Human Interaction (TOCHI), 23*(2), 1-17.

Mende, M., Scott, M. L., van Doorn, J., Grewal, D., & Shanks, I. (2019). Service robots rising: How humanoid robots influence service experiences and elicit compensatory consumer responses. *Journal of Marketing Research, 56*(4), 535-556.

Moon, Y. (2000). Intimate exchanges: Using computers to elicit self-disclosure from consumers. *Journal of Consumer Research*, *26*(4), 323-339.

Mori, M. (1970). The uncanny valley: the original essay by Masahiro Mori. *IEEE Spectrum*.

Nass, C., & Moon, Y. (2000). Machines and mindlessness: Social responses to computers. *Journal of Social Issues*, 56, 81-103.

Nass, C., & Yen, C. (2010). *The Man Who Lied to His Laptop: What We Can Learn About Ourselves from Our Machines*, Penguin Group, NY.

Pfeuffer, N., Benlian, A., Gimpel, H., & Hinz, O. (2019). Anthropomorphic information systems. *Business & Information Systems Engineering*, *61*, 523-533.

Reeves, B. & Nass, C.I. (1996), *The Media Equation*, Stanford, CA: CSLI Publications.

Waytz, A., Heafner, J., & Epley, N. (2014). The mind in the machine: Anthropomorphism increases trust in an autonomous vehicle. *Journal of Experimental Social Psychology*, *52*, 113-117.

Yalcin, G., Lim, S., Puntoni, S., & van Osselaer, S. M. (2022). Thumbs up or down: Consumer reactions to decisions by algorithms versus humans. *Journal of Marketing Research*, 59(4), 696-717.

Yeomans, M., Shah, A., Mullainathan, S., & Kleinberg, J. (2019). Making sense of recommendations. *Journal of Behavioral Decision Making, 32*(4), 403-414.

THE PERKS OF TEAMING UP WITH AI

Candrian, C., & Scherer, A. (2022). Rise of the machines: Delegating decisions to autonomous AI. *Computers in Human*

Behavior, 134, 107308.

Candrian, C., & Scherer, A. (2023). Reactance to Human versus Artificial Intelligence: Why Positive and Negative Information from Human and Artificial Agents leads to Different Responses. SSRN Electronic Journal.

Cheng, M. (2022). The Creativity of Artificial Intelligence in Art. In *Proceedings* (Vol. 81, No. 1, p. 110). MDPI.

Davenport, T. H., & Mittal, N. (2022, November 14). *How Generative AI Is Changing Creative Work*. Harvard Business Review. https://hbr.org/2022/11/how-generative-ai-is-changing-creative-work

Häubl, G., & Trifts, V. (2000). Consumer decision making in online shopping environments: The effects of interactive decision aids. *Marketing Science, 19*(1), 4-21.

Heikkilä, M. (2022, September 16). *This artist is dominating AI-generated art. And he's not happy about it.* MIT Technology Review: https://www.technologyreview.com/2022/09/16/1059598/this-artist-is-dominating-ai-generated-art-and-hes-not-happy-about-it/

Herrmann, P. N., Kundisch, D. O., & Rahman, M. S. (2015). Beating irrationality: does delegating to IT alleviate the sunk cost effect?. *Management Science, 61*(4), 831-850.

Johnson, E. J., & Payne, J. W. (1985). Effort and accuracy in choice. *Management Science, 31*(4), 395-414.

Karimi, P., Rezwana, J., Siddiqui, S., Maher, M. L., & Dehbozorgi, N. (2020, March). Creative sketching partner: an analysis of human-AI co-creativity. In *Proceedings of the 25th International Conference on Intelligent User Interfaces* (pp. 221-230).

Kim, S., Chen, R. P., & Zhang, K. (2016). Anthropomorphized helpers undermine autonomy and enjoyment in computer games. *Journal of Consumer Research, 43*(2), 282-302.

Köbis, N., & Mossink, L. D. (2021). Artificial intelligence versus Maya Angelou: Experimental evidence that people cannot differentiate AI-generated from human-written poetry. *Computers in Human Behavior, 114*, 106553.

Moutsiana, C., Garrett, N., Clarke, R. C., Lotto, R. B., Blakemore, S. J., & Sharot, T. (2013). Human development of the ability to learn from bad news. *Proceedings of the National Academy of Sciences, 110*(41), 16396-16401.

Nisbett, R. E., Ross, L. (1980). *Human Inference: Strategies and Shortcomings of Social Judgment.* Vereinigtes Königreich: Prentice-Hall.

Payne, J. W., Payne, J. W., Bettman, J. R., & Johnson, E. J. (1993). *The adaptive decision maker.* Cambridge University Press.

Roubroeks, M., Ham, J., & Midden, C. (2011). When artificial social agents try to persuade people: The role of social agency on the occurrence of psychological reactance. *International Journal of Social Robotics, 3*, 155-165.

Sharot, T. (2011). The optimism bias. *Current biology, 21*(23), R941-R945.

Sharot, T., & Garrett, N. (2016). Forming beliefs: Why valence matters. *Trends in cognitive sciences, 20*(1), 25-33.

Tversky, A., & Kahneman, D. (1981). The framing of decisions and the psychology of choice. *Science, 211*(4481), 453-458.

THE BIG BUT: THE DOWNSIDES OF TEAMING UP WITH "RATIONAL AI"

Caliskan, A., Bryson, J. J., & Narayanan, A. (2017). Semantics derived automatically from language corpora contain human-like biases. *Science, 356*(6334), 183-186.

Carr, N. G. (2015). *The glass cage: how our computers are changing us.* W.W. Norton & Company.

Dezfouli, A., Nock, R., & Dayan, P. (2020). Adversarial vulnerabilities of human decision-making. *Proceedings of the National Academy of Sciences*, 117(46), 29221-29228.

Dressel, J., & Farid, H. (2018). The accuracy, fairness, and limits of predicting recidivism. *Science Advances*, 4(1), DOI: 10.1126/sciadv.aao5580.

Flores, A. W., Bechtel, K., & Lowenkamp, C. T. (2016). False positives, false negatives, and false analyses: A rejoinder to machine bias: There's software used across the country to predict future criminals. and it's biased against blacks. Fed. Probation, 80, 38.

Henkel, L. A. (2014). Point-and-shoot memories: The influence of taking photos on memory for a museum tour. *Psychological Science*, *25*(2), 396-402.

Jago, A. S., & Laurin, K. (2022). Assumptions about algorithms' capacity for discrimination. *Personality and Social Psychology Bulletin*, 48(4), 582-595.

Kaluža, J. (2022). Habitual Generation of Filter Bubbles: Why is Algorithmic Personalisation Problematic for the Democratic Public Sphere?. *Javnost-The Public*, 1-17.

Lambrecht, A., & Tucker, C. (2019). Algorithmic bias? An empirical study of apparent gender-based discrimination in the display of STEM career ads. *Management Science*, *65*(7), 2966-2981.

Obermeyer, Z., Powers, B., Vogeli, C., & Mullainathan, S. (2019). Dissecting racial bias in an algorithm used to manage the health of populations. *Science*, *366*(6464), 447-453.

Pariser, E. (2012). *The filter bubble: how the new personalized web is changing what we read and how we think*. Penguin Books.

Rafner, J., Dellermann, D., Hjorth, A., Verasztó, D., Kampf, C., Mackay, W., & Sherson, J. (2022). Deskilling, Upskilling, and Reskilling: a Case for Hybrid Intelligence. *Morals & Machines*, *1*(2), 24-39.

Sparrow, B., Liu, J., & Wegner, D. M. (2011). Google effects on memory: Cognitive consequences of having information at our fingertips. *Science, 333*(6043), 776-778.

Susser, D., Roessler, B., & Nissenbaum, H. (2019). Online manipulation: Hidden influences in a digital world. *Geo. L. Tech. Rev., 4*, 1.

Thurman, N. (2011). Making 'The Daily Me': Technology, economics and habit in the mainstream assimilation of personalized news. *Journalism, 12*(4), 395-415.

Traeger, M. L., Strohkorb Sebo, S., Jung, M., Scassellati, B., & Christakis, N. A. (2020). Vulnerable robots positively shape human conversational dynamics in a human–robot team. *Proceedings of the National Academy of Sciences*, 117(12), 6370-6375.

Tufekci, Z. (2018, March 10). *YouTube, the Great Radicalizer.* The New York Times. https://www.nytimes.com/2018/03/10/opinion/sunday/youtube-politics-radical.html

Turkle, S. (2011). *Alone together: Why we expect more from technology and less from each other.* Basic Books.

Waytz, A. (2019). *The power of human: How our shared humanity can help us create a better world.* W. W. Norton & Company.

FEEDING AI: WHY YOUR DATA IS THE NEW HAPPY MEAL FOR AI

Acquisti, A., Brandimarte, L., & Loewenstein, G. (2020). Secrets and Likes: The Drive for Privacy and the Difficulty of Achieving It in the Digital Age. *Journal of Consumer Psychology, 30*(4), 736–758. https://doi.org/10.1002/jcpy.1191

Athey, S., Catalini, C., & Tucker, C. (2018). The Digital Privacy Paradox. *MIT Sloan Research Paper No. 5196-17, Stanford University Graduate School of Business Research Paper No. 17-14.* https://doi.org/http://dx.doi.org/10.2139/ssrn.2916489

Brehm, Sharon S and Jack W. Brehm (1981), *Psychological reactance: A theory of freedom and control.* Academic Press.

Büchi, M., Fosch-Villaronga, E., Lutz, C., Tamò-Larrieux, A., & Velidi, S. (2021). Making sense of algorithmic profiling: user perceptions on Facebook. *Information, Communication & Society*, 1-17.

Dehouche, N., & Dehouche, K. (2023). What is in a Text-to-Image Prompt: The Potential of Stable Diffusion in Visual Arts Education. *arXiv preprint arXiv:2301.01902.*

Dezfouli, A., Nock, R., & Dayan, P. (2020). Adversarial vulnerabilities of human decision-making. *Proceedings of the National Academy of Sciences, 117*(46), 29221-29228.

Hillebrand, K., & Hornuf, L. (2021). The Social Dilemma of Big Data: Donating Personal

Data to Promote Social Welfare. *SSRN Electronic Journal.*

John, L. K. (2018). Uninformed consent. *Harvard Business Review.* https://hbr.org/2018/09/uninformed-consent

Kosinski, M., Stillwell, D., & Graepel, T. (2013). Private traits and attributes are predictable from digital records of human behavior. *Proceedings of the National Academy of Sciences, 110*(15), 5802–5805.

Linek, S. B., Fecher, B., Friesike, S., & Hebing, M. (2017). Data sharing as social dilemma: Influence of the researcher's personality. *PloS one, 12*(8), e0183216.

Matz, S. C., Kosinski, M., Nave, G., & Stillwell, D. J. (2017). Psychological targeting as an effective approach to digital mass persuasion. *Proceedings of the National Academy of Sciences, 114*(48), 12714-12719.

MIT Technology Review. (2023, January 26). *How Roomba tester's private images ended up on Facebook.* https://www.technologyreview.com/2023/01/26/1067317/podcast-roomba-irobot-robot-vacuums-artificial-intelligence-training-data-privacy-consent-agreement-misled/

Nissenbaum, H. (2010). *Privacy in context: Technology, policy, and the integrity of social life.* Stanford University Press.

Puntoni, S., Reczek, R. W., Giesler, M., & Botti, S. (2021). Consumers and artificial intelligence: An experiential perspective. *Journal of Marketing, 85*(1), 131-151.

Skatova, A., & Goulding, J. (2019). Psychology of personal data donation. *PloS one, 14*(11), 1–20. https://doi.org/10.1371/journal.pone.0224240

United Nations. (2020). *Big Data for Sustainable Development.* https://www.un.org/en/global-issues/big-data-for-sustainable-development

Wenzel, C., & Scherer, A. (2022). *Sharing Data for Social Good: From Uninformed Consent to Misinformed Dissent.* SSRN Electronic Journal.

PERFECT WORLD OR PERFECT STORM? GUARDRAILS TO MAKE AI GOOD

Awad, E., Dsouza, S., Kim, R., Schulz, J., Henrich, J., Shariff, A., ... & Rahwan, I. (2018). The moral machine experiment. *Nature, 563*(7729), 59-64.

Barocas, S., Hardt, M., & Narayanan, A. (2017). *Fairness in machine learning.* Nips tutorial, 1, 2017.

Christian, B. (2020). *The alignment problem: Machine learning and human values.* W. W. Norton & Company.

Dwivedi, Y. K., Hughes, L., Ismagilova, E., Aarts, G., Coombs, C., Crick, T., ... & Williams, M. D. (2021). Artificial Intelligence (AI): Multidisciplinary perspectives on emerging challenges, opportunities, and agenda for research, practice and policy. *International Journal of Information Management, 57*, 101994.

Gordon, C. (2022, December 28). *2023 Will Be The Year Of AI Ethics Legislation Acceleration.* Forbes. https://www.forbes.

com/sites/cindygordon/2022/12/28/2023-will-be-the-ye-ar-of-ai-ethics-legislation-acceleration/?sh=101945c8e855

Gordon, C. & Upadhyay, M.A. (2021). *The AI Dilemma: A Leadership Guide to Assess Enterprise AI Maturity & Explore AI's Impact in Your Industry*. BPB Publications.

Hindriks, F., & Veluwenkamp, H. (2023). The risks of auton-omous machines: from responsibility gaps to control gaps. *Synthese*, *201*(1). https://doi.org/10.1007/s11229-022-04001-5

Korteling, J. H., van de Boer-Visschedijk, G. C., Blankend-aal, R. A., Boonekamp, R. C., & Eikelboom, A. R. (2021). Human-versus artificial intelligence. *Frontiers in artificial intelligence*, *4*, 622364.

Langston, J. (2015, April 9). *Who's a CEO? Google image results can shift gender biases*. UW News. https://www.washington.edu/news/2015/04/09/whos-a-ceo-google-image-results-can-shift-gender-biases/

Miller, T. (2019). Explanation in artificial intelligence: Insights from the social sciences. *Artificial intelligence*, *267*, 1-38.

Rai, A. (2020). Explainable AI: From black box to glass box. *Journal of the Academy of Marketing Science*, *48*, 137-141.

Taddeo, M., & Floridi, L. (2018). How AI can be a force for good. *Science*, *361*(6404), 751-752.

YOU AND AI: HOW TO MAKE IT A MATCH MADE IN HEAVEN

Roser, M. (2022, December 15). *Artificial intelligence is trans-forming our world — it is on all of us to make sure that it goes well*. Our World in Data. https://ourworldindata.org/ai-impact

Taddeo, M., & Floridi, L. (2018). How AI can be a force for

good. *Science, 361*(6404), 751-752.

Tegmark, M. (2018). *Life 3.0: Being human in the age of artificial intelligence.* Vintage.

ABOUT THE AUTHORS

Anne Scherer is a true pioneer in the fields of consumer psychology and technology. For over a decade, she has been on a mission to discover how new technologies are transforming the way we interact with businesses. As an Assistant Professor of Quantitative Marketing at the University of Zurich and co-founder of Delta Labs AG, Anne delves deep into the fascinating world of AI, robo-advisors, and conversational interfaces.

Driven by her passion for "better tech," Anne supports startups, companies, and NGOs in shaping our AI-driven future. She has been a member of the World Economic Forum's Global Future Councils and is known for her groundbreaking research, published in top academic journals and major media outlets. Her TEDxTalk, in which she discusses why we are more honest with machines, has already been viewed over 1.8 million times.

Before joining the University of Zurich, Anne conducted research at ETH Zurich and earned her PhD with honors from the Technical University of Munich.

Anne is not only a scientist but also a true adventurer. She has traveled the world, from diving in the Red Sea to cycling on Easter Island, and these experiences have enriched her perspective. In this way, Anne contributes to shaping a technology-driven future that is as exciting as her own adventures. Anne lives with her partner in Zurich.

Cindy Candrian is not only a gifted AI expert and entrepreneur, but also a true advocate of the human factor and quantitative methods. With her PhD from the University of Zurich, she embarked on an exciting journey to explore how data and technology can improve our decision-making. Her groundbreaking findings have made their way into prestigious journals such as Computers in Human Behavior and have been presented at academic conferences worldwide.

In her role as a serial entrepreneur, Cindy has launched two successful startups – her latest venture being Delta Labs AG. At Delta Labs, her main goal is to develop innovative and tailored AI solutions for businesses by employing cutting-edge methods and algorithms. She is particularly enthusiastic about "hybrid intelligence" and how AI can enhance and complement human work.

Outside of her professional life, Cindy is a talented hobby designer and created all the impressive images in this book using DALL-E. She is also passionate about extensive hikes through the Swiss mountains, accompanied by her loyal four-legged companion, Benji. These nature experiences inspire her and provide new energy for her creative projects. Together with her partner and Benji, Cindy lives in an idyllic municipality near Zurich, continuing to make her mark in the world of AI and data-driven decision-making.